Mixed Methods Research

POCKET GUIDES TO
SOCIAL WORK RESEARCH METHODS

Series Editor

Tony Tripodi, DSW
Professor Emeritus, Ohio State University

DAPHNE C. WATKINS
DEBORAH GIOIA

Mixed Methods Research

OXFORD
UNIVERSITY PRESS

OXFORD
UNIVERSITY PRESS

Oxford University Press is a department of the University of
Oxford. It furthers the University's objective of excellence in research,
scholarship, and education by publishing worldwide.

Oxford   New York
Auckland   Cape Town   Dar es Salaam   Hong Kong   Karachi
Kuala Lumpur   Madrid   Melbourne   Mexico City   Nairobi
New Delhi   Shanghai   Taipei   Toronto

With offices in
Argentina   Austria   Brazil   Chile   Czech Republic   France   Greece
Guatemala   Hungary   Italy   Japan   Poland   Portugal   Singapore
South Korea   Switzerland   Thailand   Turkey   Ukraine   Vietnam

Oxford is a registered trademark of Oxford University Press
in the UK and certain other countries.

Published in the United States of America by
Oxford University Press
198 Madison Avenue, New York, NY 10016

© Oxford University Press 2015

All rights reserved. No part of this publication may be reproduced, stored in
a retrieval system, or transmitted, in any form or by any means, without the prior
permission in writing of Oxford University Press, or as expressly permitted by law,
by license, or under terms agreed with the appropriate reproduction rights organization.
Inquiries concerning reproduction outside the scope of the above should be sent to the
Rights Department, Oxford University Press, at the address above.

You must not circulate this work in any other form
and you must impose this same condition on any acquirer.

Library of Congress Cataloging-in-Publication Data
Daphne C. Watkins
Mixed Methods Research / Daphne C. Watkins, Deborah Gioia.
pages cm. — (Pocket guides to social work research methods)
Includes bibliographical references and index.
ISBN 978-0-19-974745-0 (paperback)
1. Social service—Research.   2. Research—Methodology.
I. Deborah Gioia.   II. Title.
HV11.W38 2015
001.4′2—dc23
2015003389

Contents

Preface

The definition of mixed methods is varied, still a work in progress, and touches on issues of mixing philosophies of science as well as method. The recent growth of mixed methods research in social work and elsewhere is the result of several factors, including the influx of publications on mixed methods and the increased use of qualitative data analysis software. Despite this, however, we think that the increased need for scholars to grapple with the multiple facets that individuals and communities are facing is probably the most important reason for the increase in the inquiry, interest, and application of mixed methods research. For example, mixed methods research has enormous potential for assisting scholars in tackling the complex questions that impact the health and well-being of individuals whose lives are impacted by the intersectional factors of social and economic influences. This is certainly the case for social workers, whose preamble in the National Association for Social Workers (2014) states:

> Social workers are sensitive to cultural and ethnic diversity and strive to end discrimination, oppression, poverty, and other forms of social injustice. These activities may be in the form of direct practice, community organizing, supervision, consultation administration, advocacy,

social and political action, policy development and implementation, education, and *research* and evaluation. (Emphasis added)

Mixed methods studies require multiple inputs of expertise and effort (Padgett, 2009). In a guest editorial Padgett urges researchers in social work who use qualitative methods to recognize and interrogate our epistemological approach to our research, to be mindful of the rigor needed in all phases of the research process in order to report trustworthy findings, to be consistent in the approaches we choose when designing our studies and the dissemination of the findings, and to not sideline our theories or social justice concerns, which are core components of social work. Often when we embark on research enterprises with our colleagues from other disciplines, they are amazed at the attention that we give to the theoretical underpinnings of the research, as well as the importance of the bio/psycho/social/spiritual context of our participants. These interdisciplinary "aha" moments are golden, as they allow us to bring our disciplinary expertise into the research arena where we will inevitably be working with others on these complex problems.

Mixed methods provide statistics and stories that complement and contrast to inform our thinking about the problems at hand. For example, one day a colleague was discussing a large-scale poverty study and was very excited when the creation of a new variable—food insufficiency—arose in their team process as necessary to explain the struggles people had with making enough money to buy food that would last all month. A qualitative researcher would likely want to interview people about this stressful life event and try to understand the strategies employed to deal with lack of food. A qualitative researcher would want to contextualize the food insufficiency experience with rich descriptions from the participants. On the other hand, a quantitative researcher would want to understand the prevalence of food insufficiency between and within groups in the sample and make certain that the interview guide probed areas of inequity and injustice as related to the food insufficiency. The quantitative researcher may also want to know how closely food insufficiency is tied to inadequacy in the public system established for the care of the poor. Practically speaking, a mixed methods researcher would want access to all of these, and a mixed methods researcher in social work would also want to know how access to the this information would lead to change in the community. This is the beginning of a mixed way of thinking about research, and it is "a research paradigm whose time has come" (Johnson & Onwuegbuzie, 2004, p. 14). Every human problem that social work researchers explore is a complex problem, and this text will help us to adopt a mixed methods way of thinking about problems even if we make a design decision to choose qualitative or qualitative only (Greene, 2007).

The overall rationale for mixing methods in social inquiry is for a "better understanding" of the inherent complexities of human phenomena. Better understanding, mixed methods advocates maintain, can be importantly attained by using all of our ways of knowing and understanding (Greene, 2007). No one approach is privileged over the other in this understanding, despite the tension we may feel as a profession in research related to evidence-based practices and interventions where a randomized control trial is the gold standard. The truth of real-world research in social work is that very few of us will engage in random control trial research, and so it would appear that an alternate approach to strengthening our studies might be a well-developed mixed methods study. As social workers, we look at the cumulative burdens of our clients—posttraumatic stress disorder, chronic pain, depression, unemployment, social difficulties—and since complexity within the context matters, we should bring our science in to match (Malai, 2012).

In order to nest mixed methods squarely within the social work domain, this text first makes the argument about the nature of our *science* in social work (i.e., biopsychosocial perspective), our branding, what we are known for. We reference a Brekke (2012) article on translational science in *Research on Social Work Practice* to help the reader understand why a mixed methods design in studies might tease out more of the complexities and nudge the process of dissemination of interventions to our constituencies in a more expedient manner. Implementing clinical (and other) interventions into daily life practices is remarkably slow and inefficient and may take 17 to 20 years to have research results manifest in the community (Balas & Boren, 2000). It would be very difficult to look community participants in the eye and tell them that very little benefit will come to them in the immediate future from their willingness to serve science. While mixed methods are not a panacea for improving this outlandish delay, use of mixed methods may serve to deepen our [personal] insights as we attempt to answer very complicated research questions (Sandelowski, 2000), bring richer data to stakeholders, and ultimately bring about treatments and services to people who need them (Brekke, 2012).

All mixed methods studies, by definition, attempt some form of integration (Bazeley, 2009). We define integration in mixed methods as the linkage between qualitative and quantitative data based on a predetermined system that helps determine how we gain knowledge. Integration is a benchmark that will resonate throughout this text and a goal to pursue when complications arise in defining mixed methods research. A cause for concern is that studies using qualitative or mixed methods may be conceptually and methodologically very weak and include minimal attempts at integration. This text attempts to contribute to a basic understanding about mixed methods studies so that when they are employed, they are done well.

Colleagues and students engaged in theses, dissertations, and early career mixed methods research will find this text especially useful. A study in the *British Journal of Social Work* reported that the majority of dissertations reviewed reported using qualitative or mixed methods research, with only 5% reporting to have completed a quantitative-only study (Scourfield & Maxwell, 2010). However, even in the quantitative studies, descriptive and bivariate statistics were the overwhelming choice, with little attempt to integrate the data sets. Drisko (2000) was equally critical of qualitative data analysis standards and rigor in journal articles accepted in US publications in the 1990s. It is also possible that some parts of the data were analyzed and published sooner than the others—bringing community results to the stakeholders faster. Bryman (2007) analyzed 20 mixed methods studies in the United Kingdom and identified multiple barriers to the integration of data. This evidence clearly suggests that if we are to move more competently into producing high-quality mixed methods studies, we require a primer in the processes and logic of this undertaking. This text is a first step in encouraging doctoral students and others to engage in and strengthen their expertise in the strategies required to engage in mixed method research and contribute to the larger interdisciplinary discussion about what form this hybrid will take within and beyond social work.

ABOUT THE AUTHORS

Daphne C. Watkins became interested in mixed methods research in her quest to uncover the "voices behind the numbers." After completing a bachelor's degree in anthropology, she entered a graduate-level health education program where she learned about advanced statistics and the benefits of research that is both inductive and deductive. Her love of anthropology (the history of mankind) and her desire to advance public health (what she would describe as "the future of mankind") motivated her to uncover ways to apply both *depth* and *breadth* in her own research on the health disparities of marginalized groups.

Watkins has taught research methods to social workers and human service professionals for more than a decade. From the very beginning, she recognized the importance of including both quantitative and qualitative methods in courses and reworked the syllabi for her basic social work research classes so that they would reflect the true nature of social work research. Also, after noticing the lack of continuing education opportunities for social workers that focus on research, she developed and launched the Certificate Program in Mixed Methods Research through the University of Michigan School of Social Work's continuing education office in the summer of 2013. This program is designed for researchers and practitioners in social work, nursing, psychology, and other applied fields who are interested in learning ways to integrate various types of qualitative and quantitative research methods, commonly used statistical procedures, and approaches to research conducted in practice settings. In the first year, 23 participants enrolled in the five-week program and learned how to understand and appreciate the science behind mixed methods approaches to building practice knowledge. The program is designed such that special emphasis is placed on increasing participants' abilities to critique theoretical foundations of research, form research questions, apply mixed methods research techniques, conduct statistical analyses, integrate qualitative and quantitative data, and interpret mixed methods research reports.

To date, all of Watkins' primary research studies have been qualitative, quantitative, or mixed methods in nature. Her first mixed methods project was her dissertation research on Black college men and mental health. In this study, Watkins examined Black college men at a predominately White university and a historically Black college/university and collected both qualitative (i.e., focus groups) and quantitative (i.e., survey data) from the men (Watkins, 2006; Watkins, Green, Goodson, Guidry, & Stanley, 2007; Watkins & Neighbors, 2007). During the data integration phase of her study, she found that the qualitative results were not supported (i.e., confirmed) by the quantitative results. In other words, the survey data reported one aspect of the findings that was not supported by (and was in fact contradictory to) the focus group findings. Since completing her doctoral studies, Watkins' research has focused on using mixed methods to understand the social determinants of health that explain within-group differences among Black men, developing evidence-based strategies to improve the physical and mental health of Black men, and increasing knowledge about the intersection of culture, ethnicity, age, and gender (a selection of her publications are listed in the References).

Deborah Gioia has a background and sensitizing experiences for engaging in mixed methods research that emanate from several sources. First, her 20+ years' experience as a licensed clinical social worker employed in a National Institute of Mental Health funded longitudinal protocol at the University of California Los Angeles exploring the onset and trajectory of schizophrenia in the lives of young adults was the fertile field for her philosophical and methodological position. She was trained on multiple, individual, and family psychological assessment measures and subjected to periodic fidelity checks. It was important for her to understand and translate the findings as a team member of this national project.

In her doctoral program at the University of Southern California, she was trained in basic quantitative data analysis and management skills, but it was her exposure to qualitative research methods that was most compelling and reinforced her notions that answering her research questions would best be handled with static measures of her partici-pants' symptom levels and quality of life measures, plus rich, in-depth interviews and observations that would allow participants to imbue that data with meaning. In the summer of 2004 she co-led with Dr. Deborah Padgett the first National Institutes of Health–sponsored week-long institute, The Design and Conduct of Qualitative and Mixed-Method Research in Social Work and Other Health Professions, which was attended mainly by social work doctoral students and faculty, as well as nursing students and faculty. She has been teaching qualitative research methods to doctoral students at the University of Maryland, Baltimore for the past seven years and is also planning a one-credit mixed methods seminar for doctoral students. All of Gioia's studies have utilized mixed methods. A selection of her publications is listed below:

Gioia, D. (2006a). A contextual study of daily living strategies in neurocognitively impaired adults with schizophrenia. *Qualitative Health Research, 16*(9), 1217–1235.

Gioia, D. (2006b). Examining work delay in young adults with schizophrenia. *American Journal of Psychiatric Rehabilitation, 9*(3), 167–190.

Gioia, D., & Brekke, J. S. (2009). Neurocognition, ecological validity, and daily living in the community for individuals with schizophrenia: A mixed methods study. *Psychiatry: Interpersonal and Biological Processes, 72*(1), 93–106.

RATIONALE FOR THIS TEXT

Over the years, we have not only witnessed the challenges associated with learning mixed methods research, but we have also experienced them for ourselves. We understand the challenge with trying to learn and navigate a research approach that is still emerging. Therefore we felt that a primer on mixed methods research would be useful for students, colleagues, and more seasoned social work professionals. Our hope for readers is that they will benefit from the way we have organized this text, which includes nine steps toward planning, implementing, and interpreting mixed methods research in social work.

Mixed method studies demand that we apply sound analytic strategies to all our evidence—qualitative and quantitative. This book covers (a) mixed methods research in a concise manner, (b) how mixed methods (qualitative and quantitative) within the same study are being used in social work research, and (c) the unique possibilities for the future of mixed methods in social work. Our combined teaching and research experience with mixed methods spans two decades. Over the years, we both have had experience teaching research methods to social workers. Our previous classes have been quantitative, qualitative, and mixed methods in nature and have been taught in classroom settings and via the Internet.

The *Journal of Mixed Methods Research* launched in January 2007 and has been a grand attempt to cull the best displays of data integration while staying open to the different conceptualizations and definitions that each researcher brings to mixed methods (Tashakkori & Creswell, 2007a, 2007b). Also, we both recently returned from the inaugural conference of the Mixed Methods International Research Association (MMIRA) that was held in Boston, Massachusetts. According to the MMIRA (Mertens, 2014) website (http://mmira.wildapricot.org/):

> The Mixed Methods International Research Association (MMIRA) aims to create an international community to promote interdisciplinary mixed methods research. The mission of the Association is to engage with the international community to support mixed methods research, which broadly includes the following: mixing/ combining/ integrating quantitative and/ or qualitative methods, epistemologies, axiologies, and stakeholder perspectives and standpoints.
>
> MMIRA seeks to engage with a broad set of approaches in the service of understanding complex social, behavioral, health, educational, and political concerns related to the human condition and natural world. Our vision includes bringing together diverse communities of scholars, students, practitioners, policymakers, citizens, and other stakeholders, with the goals of expanding knowledge and producing social betterment and social and global justice.

What we appreciated most about our attendance at the MMIRA conference was our ability to interact with mixed methods researchers from all disciplines, professions, and parts of the world. Our participation in this meeting truly illuminated our enthusiasm for how far we have come in mixed methods, with an equally exciting expectation for what is to come.

ABOUT THIS TEXT

It would seem that regardless of whether we use a single method or mixed methods, we begin each study by assessing, weighing, and using available and appropriate methods to explore our topic and end with some type of explanation of phenomena, depending on the purpose of the research. What happens in between is varied, and these decisions are worthy of a study of their own. This text touches on how each researcher should establish his or her own mixed methods research philosophy and how one should view the investigation of truth in general, and within one's own research domain, so as to converse with others about what is foundational to one's own research career. These are core ingredients of what we set out to do—to have a conversation about our area of social work research in the context of mixed methods.

Given our early twenty-first-century context, we as social workers understand that social problems are complex and call for more creative uses of available methods in research studies. This foundational notion may be what leads us to mixed methods in the first place. Given the ethics and imperatives of our discipline of social work, we understand that research is pursued through relationships, and we are called upon in our research to consider the same values that we do in our work with individuals, communities, and groups. This is an important part of our worldview. The core values of the social work profession are service, social justice, dignity and worth of the person, importance of human relationships, integrity, and competence.

In 2007 David Morgan suggested that advocates for qualitative research became part of the scientific landscape from the 1960s forward and that this was the first step toward a shift in paradigms and a chance for the evolution of mixed methods research to occur. So how do we take what some researchers feel cannot be done—integrate qualitative and quantitative data in one study—and attempt to understand this difficult process, replete with its differing worldviews and assumptions, in order to garner new understanding about our research problem? These concerns are elaborated on in each of the chapters that follow—and all of this will be done in the context of the social work profession. How and why do mixed methods matter for social work researchers? Is theory essential to incorporate in our mixed methods studies in social work? And is there something particular in the nature of our *science* in social work (i.e., the bio-psychosocial-spiritual perspective) that is conducive to incorporating mixed methods approaches for our research questions (Brekke, 2012; Evans, Coon, & Ume, 2011; Longhofer & Floersch, 2012; Thyer, 2001)?

When we have had the opportunity to meet with Dr. John Creswell (a prominent voice in the mixed methods landscape) over the years, our conversations would inevitably seem to arrive at a question of great importance for him, and one that we try and be faithful to in this text. He would tell us about being invited to give mixed methods talks and trainings across a wide range of disciplines, from nursing to pharmacy, occupational therapy to social work. Everyone seemed to want his expertise, but what he could not tell these groups was whether mixed methods looked different in different disciplines. As an educational psychologist, Creswell could appreciate his use of the methods and the designs he developed to incorporate the mix of qualitative and quantitative data in his discipline, but he also understood that data strategies would change with their adoption by other disciplines and cultures. Knowing how the methods changed within disciplines is what he was counting on others to do, as well as report on in journal articles and at conferences the manner in which these changes occurred. In this text, we aim to (a) tackle some of the challenges associated with adopting mixed methods in social work and (b) frame mixed methods in the professional and disciplinary context of social work.

GOALS OF THIS TEXT

This text has the following goals: first, we review the fundamentals of mixed methods research designs and the general suppositions of mixed methods procedures that have been developed broadly. Second, we look critically at mixed method studies and models that have already been employed in social work and reflect on the contributions of this work to our field. Finally, we consider the application of the mixed methods research in social work settings. The chapters of this book are structured so that interested social workers can use it as a practical guide for conducting mixed methods research in social work settings. This text is meant to (figuratively) "walk" the reader through the mixed methods research process using nine steps (and six "floors," or book chapters). Chapters 1, 5, and 6 provide material meant to serve as supplemental content for chapters 2, 3, and 4, which outline the nine steps in the mixed methods research process, specific to social work research.

HOW TO READ THIS TEXT

The information in this text is presented sequentially; however, readers may choose to skip certain chapters for now and return to them at a later date. Although the content of each chapter is self-contained, we encourage readers to review each chapter in the order in which they are presented, as each chapter builds on the one that precedes it. Chapter 1 of this text provides an introduction to a "mixed" way of thinking. Chapter 2 is about designing mixed methods studies in social work and is divided into the first three steps of the mixed methods research process: Step 1: Developing mixed methods purpose statements of research questions; Step 2: Understanding mixed methods design notation and language; and Step 3: Choosing a mixed methods design. Chapter 3 covers mixed methods data collection and includes Steps 4 through 6 of the mixed methods research process: Step 4: Deciding on the data collection methods; Step 5: Developing a sampling plan and recruitment strategies; and Step 6: Collecting the data. Chapter 4 covers the final steps in the mixed methods research process, which encompasses data analysis and interpretation of the findings: Step 7: Preparing the data for analysis; Step 8: Analyzing the data; and Step 9: Interpreting and presenting findings. Chapter 5 presents the perils, pitfalls, and additional considerations of mixed methods research that are specific to social workers. We also have included some exemplar mixed methods studies in chapter 5 as models for our readers. Finally, chapter 6 discusses important elements involved in writing up, presenting, and teaching mixed methods.

Acknowledgments

There are many individuals who have made the process of writing this book possible. Some people have contributed to our development as researchers in the form of direct mentoring—teaching us about the processes and practices involved in qualitative, quantitative, and mixed methods research. Some have been advocates for us to take the next steps in writing a mixed methods text for social work, based on our knowledge and understanding of the discipline-specific issues that may be encountered by social work researchers. We first acknowledge our editor, Dana Bliss, for his support and patience as this book project evolved over time. We also thank Deborah Padgett, who has been both a teacher and an advocate for qualitative research and for our development. Next, we acknowledge John W. Creswell, who has been an inspirational teacher through his many texts, workshops, and conferences that we have attended. In conversations, dating back almost a decade, he laid out the grand challenge about the place of mixed methods in social work research. He provided strong encouragement and confidence that we could have a role in that conversation and emphasized that a book on mixed methods research in social work was needed. We also thank our mentors and colleagues who provided encouragement and support and agreed that such a mixed methods text in social work was needed: Laura Lein, Jorge Delva, Ruth Dunkle, Michael Spencer, John Brekke,

Vicki L. Plano Clark, Michael Fetters, Mary Ruffolo, Linda Chatters, Robert Joseph Taylor, Donna Harrington, Helen C. Kales, B. Lee Green, Jamie Abelson, Joe Gallo, and Jamie Mitchell. We would also like to thank the students from our classes and research groups (i.e., the University of Michigan Gender and Health Research Lab) who, over the years, have made us better teachers. Finally, the formatting and polishing of this book would not have been completed in a timely fashion without the assistance of Michelle Jendry and the support from our friends and loved ones.

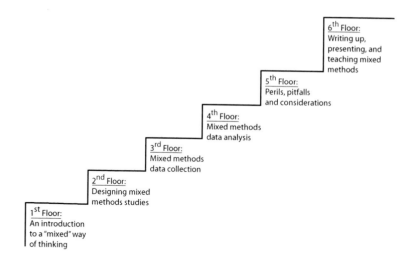

Mixed Methods Research in Social Work: A Visual Depiction of the Pocket Guide Steps (Each "floor" represents a chapter)

Mixed Methods Research

1

"First Floor": An Introduction to a "Mixed" Way of Thinking

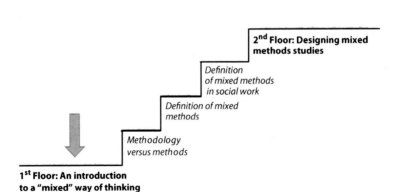

2nd **Floor: Designing mixed methods studies**

Definition of mixed methods in social work

Definition of mixed methods

Methodology versus methods

1st **Floor: An introduction to a "mixed" way of thinking**

This chapter describes the lay of the land of mixed methods. Whenever possible some illustrative examples are used from published, peer-reviewed sources. This chapter does not go extensively into the mixed methods paradigm debate, as these discussions can be found in other sources (Creswell, 2015; Creswell & Plano Clark, 2011; Greene, 2002; Maxwell & Loomis, 2003; Mayoh & Onwuegbuzie, 2013). Moreover, in the spirit of introducing a "mixed" way of thinking, we begin with a discussion of the difference between *method* and *methodology* for both quantitative and qualitative research. Next we offer and frame a definition of mixed methods in social work, complete within the context of a social justice framework. Finally, we end this chapter with an outline of the nine steps for mixed methods research in social work.

INTRODUCTION

Understanding what defines a mixed methods study is a relatively recent (approximately 25 years) and emerging trend, although we have guidance from many scholars across numerous disciplines and two editions of two major handbooks: *SAGE Handbook of Mixed Methods in Social & Behavioral Research* (Tashakkori & Teddlie, 2010; first edition, 2003) and *Designing and Conducting Mixed Methods Research* (Creswell & Plano Clark, 2011; first edition, 2007). But there is still much more to explore. A major review in sociology on mixed methods research acknowledges that there are both promising innovations in this area and methodological uncertainties, but recent decades have brought a great deal of attention to the scope, justification for, and challenges to this methodology (Small, 2011). Additionally, this major review makes the point that there are numerous disciplines utilizing mixed methods that have developed their own literatures and justifications, often without consulting what has already been developed in other areas. In order to frame social work's position and definition of mixed methods, we first describe two commonly (and erroneously) misused research terms: *methodology* and *method*.

METHODOLOGY VERSUS METHOD

The terms *methodology* and *method* are not synonymous, although they are often treated as such. *Methodology* is a lens through which research is examined. By virtue of methodology's positioning in social work, it is oftentimes (by default) also how we see the world. The reason scholars may adhere to a particular methodology to address a research problem oftentimes has more to do with the scholar's perspective on the world. For example, a scholar who values the contribution that statistics make to understanding a problem may see the world through a positivist (i.e., explanatory) lens. Although the scholar may still value words and experiences in context (i.e., positivism), he or she may tend to lean toward positivism (at least initially) when attempting to solve a research problem. Although related, methods are not the same as methodology. *Methods* are the techniques that are used to confirm the methodological underpinning in a study. In other words, if methodology is the theory behind the research, then methods are the tools used to collect the information needed to understand (either confirm or contradict) the research. See Hesse-Biber's (2010) work for a detailed explanation of the difference between methodology and methods. However, for the purposes of this text, we suggest that readers think about the ordering of methods and methodology in the research process in the way in which we have outlined it in Figure 1.1: methodology, research questions, methods, and data.

Hesse-Biber (2010) notes that "methods lie in the service of methodologies" (p. 13). Similarly, when it comes to the operationalization of methodologies and methods, we believe that Jennifer Greene (2002) captured the role of methodologies in research projects best:

> Most . . . methodologies have preferences for particular methods, but methods gain meaning only from the methodologies that share and guide their use . . . An interview does not inherently respect the agency of individual human life; it only does so if guided by and implemented within a methodological framework that advances the stance. So, any discussions of mixed methods . . . must be discussions of mixed methodologies, and thus of the complex epistemological and value-based issues that such an idea invokes. (p. 260)

Figure 1.1. The ordering of methodology, research questions, methods, and data in the research process.

As our colleagues have provided a thorough explanation of the differences between methods and methodology elsewhere, we now enter into a discussion about the methods in quantitative research and qualitative research, respectively.

QUANTITATIVE METHODS

When choosing a quantitative method, social workers should strive to minimize error and maximize the response rate. The type of quantitative data that needs to be collected will depend on the type of research question that is asked. Quantitative researchers make claims based on determinism or cause-and-effect thinking; reductionism, by narrowing and focusing on select variables to interrelate; detailed observations and measures of variables; and the testing of theories that are continually refined (Slife & Williams, 1995). Table 1.1 illustrates characteristics of quantitative research that may result in choosing some of the more popular quantitative data collection methods used in social work research such as surveys and standardized measures.

Quantitative methods stem from a positivism worldview and seek to understand the breadth of the human experience. With quantitative research, meaning is best captured with numbers and "counting things" (Watkins, 2012). Quantitative research is also highly applicable to social work due to our interest in the number of peoples' lives that are affected by an experience or a certain phenomenon.

Table 1.1. Characteristics of Quantitative Research

- Seeks a broad understanding
- Views social phenomena atomistically (i.e., using several elements)
- Provides prevalence and incidence rates of decisions and actions
- Uses closed-ended methods
- Is fixed rather than iterative
- Is preconstructed rather than emergent
- Involves respondents as subjects
- Is performed by an investigator who remains objective and is not an instrument in the research process

Strengths and Limitations of Quantitative Research

A strength of quantitative research is that it can generate a broad understanding of a phenomenon from hundreds (even thousands) of people. Also, quantitative research can sometimes be conducted faster than qualitative research because quantitative data is often more concise and can be collected using computers and other information systems. In the age of the Internet-based survey, more social work researchers are taking advantage of online survey programs to collect their client data (discussed further in chapter 3). Another strength of quantitative research is that it can help test and/or verify theory. Oftentimes social workers have practice-based knowledge that is acquired from other sources. For example, practice interventions may be based on agency culture or tradition, but perhaps the social worker implementing the intervention wants to test it in a different setting (or with a different group of clients) to evaluate its effectiveness. Perhaps the social worker's supervisor has promised some additional resources if the social worker can provide him or her with evidence that the intervention is effective across multiple settings. For a situation such as this, quantitative research can be used to test the intervention with different groups of clients. Pre- and posttest survey data can be collected from a new group of clients and compared to data from the original group of clients. Another advantage is the accessibility of quantitative data (particularly existing quantitative data, referred to as "secondary data"), which is useful in acquiring information about a group of clients without needing to collect new data (or the resources to do so).

Despite the advantages of quantitative research, it is not without its limitations. For example, quantitative research does not account for the depth that is sometimes needed to investigate social work research questions. Also, sometimes program stakeholders may want an explanation for the number of clients who did or did not participate in a program (or for those who did or did not improve at the end of the program). Because quantitative research is most commonly used in a deductive process that leads to identifying patterns of behavior, it is limited to exploring hypothetical relationships and testing theories. As such, quantitative researchers tend to focus on the measurement and analysis of exploratory, descriptive, and/or explanatory variables (Grinnell & Unrau, 2014). Both quantitative and qualitative research methods are essential to advancing what we know about the living and working conditions of people. Next we review qualitative methods.

QUALITATIVE METHODS

Qualitative methods come from the interpretive or narrative tradition, and they seek to understand deeper meanings of the human experience. By "meanings," we are referring to experiences that are best captured with words and images, rather than with numbers and counting, as we tend to do with quantitative methods (Watkins, 2012). Qualitative methods are highly applicable to social work due to our vested interest in people's lives and what it is like to experience certain phenomena. Moreover, social workers tend to choose their profession because they care about people and want to be in direct contact with them. We are not typically in a lab studying people and/or actions from a distance, but rather we are invested in what is "local" and relevant in a particular context. Qualitative methods help us to capture what that social experience is like.

Qualitative research allows us to address some of the more complicated phenomena, such as intersections of race and gender in health and well-being, by providing vivid, dense, and full descriptions of this phenomenon from the perspective of research participants (Banyard & Miller, 1998; Farquhar, Parker, Schulz, & Israel, 2006; Miles & Huberman, 1994; Watkins, 2012). Certain characteristics of qualitative research distinguish it from quantitative research (Glaser & Strauss, 1967; Lincoln & Guba, 1985; Ulin, Robinson, & Tolley, 2005; Watkins, 2012). For example, instead of answering the "what" and "how many" questions of quantitative research, qualitative research helps to address "why," "how," and "under what circumstances" things occur. Table 1.2 provides some basic characteristics of qualitative research.

Morse and Richards (2002) offer five suggestions for when qualitative methods are most appropriate. First, qualitative methods should be used when very little is known about a topic and initial exploration is needed in order to know what to study. Second, understanding a particular topic regarding a situation that is in a transitional process requires the depth of qualitative inquiry. Third, qualitative methods are needed when there is interest in studying reactions to a natural setting

Table 1.2. Characteristics of Qualitative Research

- Seeks an in-depth understanding
- Views social phenomena holistically
- Provides insight into the meanings of decisions and actions
- Uses open-ended methods
- Is iterative rather than fixed
- Is emergent rather than prestructured
- Involves respondents as active participants rather than subjects
- Acknowledges the investigator as an instrument in the research process

(or process) to determine participants' experience of it. Fourth, when the goal is to develop new theory that is grounded in reality or the lived experience, qualitative methods can be particularly useful. Finally, researchers can use qualitative methods when the research aim is to cultivate a deep understanding of certain human phenomena (Morse & Richards, 2002). Germane to all five of these suggestions is the goal of acquiring depth, understanding the human experience, and moving what we currently know about a particular phenomenon forward. Qualitative researchers assume behavior is bound to social and cultural context and focus on a more in-depth understanding of the relationship between these contexts and the phenomenon of interest.

Qualitative research is, therefore, useful in the inductive process of building theory and revealing subjective processes that result in understanding participants' behaviors (Miles & Huberman, 1994; Padgett, 2009; Watkins, 2012). These provide an umbrella under which qualitative methods should be utilized. Although some methods tend to be more popular than others, a scoping review of qualitative research in social work suggests that social workers tend to use case studies, ethnography, grounded theory, and phenomenology in their work. A *case study* helps us develop an understanding of a topic through an in-depth analysis of one or a few single-case examples. A case study can involve an individual, a group of people, or a single event, but the goal is to treat the "case" as a singular unit of analysis, rather than the entire sample of cases. *Ethnography* is a form of field research that focuses on understanding an entire culture or subculture through participant observation (and often) engagement. The ethnographer becomes immersed in the culture as an active participant and records extensive field notes (Watkins, 2012). *Grounded theory* is a process of inductive theory development based on intensive observation. It is an iterative process in which the researcher begins with raising broad questions and ends with construction of theoretical concepts and their relationships clearly linked by the data. *Phenomenology* focuses on people's subjective experiences and their interpretation of their world. The goal of the researcher in phenomenological research is to describe the world of the people under study from their point of view (Watkins, 2012). This involves full immersion into the lives, language, and understandings of the people under study.

Strengths and Limitations of Qualitative Methods

A strength of qualitative research is that it helps generate a rich understanding of a particular topic and of the lived experiences that are not accessible via quantitative methods. In other words, it adds an additional layer of knowledge that we cannot acquire with quantitative data. Qualitative research is highly flexible, because the data collection process is ongoing and occurs simultaneously with data analysis, allowing the research plan to be altered as needed. Qualitative research can sometimes be less expensive than quantitative research (we provide more on this in chapter 3). Some limitations of qualitative research are that it lacks generalizability because the findings are so in-depth that they speak specifically to the sample (or individual) at hand. Qualitative research is also subjective; therefore, the researchers have some influence on the findings of the study. Although bias can be reduced, it is almost never eliminated because that is the nature of qualitative inquiry: bias is made explicit.

SOCIAL WORK RESEARCH METHODS

As social work researchers, we must acknowledge the importance of the worldview and, therefore, the methodology through which we view the world. The way one sees the world influences everything about one's research, from the methodological standpoint, to the research question asked (and how it is asked), to how the data are collected, analyzed, and interpreted. Mixed methods involves more than mixing the methods; it requires mixing the assumptions that we have about the methodologies, the methods, the research questions, and the data. This is influenced by reflexivity—how we are positioned in our research affects everything about our research. We agree with Hesse-Biber's (2010) observation that mixed methods research has taken a "cart before the horse" approach in current trends (p. 10). Also, like Hesse-Biber, we agree that this is the wrong perspective to take with mixed methods research. Instead, we suggest that the research question be used as the driving force behind the decision to use mixed methods research in social work. So when is a qualitative (or quantitative) method appropriate to use? The answer to this question is simple: when a research question calls for the method to be used. We provide sample research questions and important decisions to consider in this regard later in the text.

The basic knowledge level continuum in social work research and evaluation texts (Grinnell & Unrau, 2014) teaches us that there are three types of research: exploratory, descriptive, and explanatory. With research at the exploratory level, little is known about the area, and we are often studying a particular phenomenon because we want to discover which concepts about the phenomenon are relevant. With research at the descriptive level, we are attempting to describe a phenomenon in a holistic way. Descriptive research is most concerned with the numbers: how many people, places, and things are involved and what are their characteristics, as well as what processes occur and how often they occur. With research at the explanatory level, we want to focus on "why" things happen and offer causations and predictions. Explanatory research usually helps to explain the relationship between variables, and we also use it to test social work theories (Grinnell & Unrau, 2014).

We posit that understanding the knowledge level continuum is important to understanding mixed methods in social work research. This is because a driving force of social work research is to deepen our understanding of the social injustices and inequalities of marginalized groups so that we can devise a plan of action to help them improve their social and economic situations. The knowledge level continuum provides a road map to accomplish this goal; deciding what we need to know is always a first step toward action. Whether we want to acquire knowledge that is exploratory, descriptive, explanatory, or a combination of these, the way in which we, as social workers, use that knowledge is what makes our profession one of impact and change. Oftentimes, in our decision about what we need to know, varying types of knowledge need to be obtained in order to deepen our understanding and thereby help us make a meaningful impact. This is where mixed methods can be used to advance social work research. In the following section we provide a definition of mixed methods and then frame our definition of mixed methods in the context of social work.

THE DEFINITION OF MIXED METHODS

Mixed methods research has two distinct characteristics. First, it involves the collection and analysis of qualitative and quantitative data in ways that are rigorous and epistemologically sound (Creswell, 2015; Creswell & Plano Clark, 2011; Hesse-Biber, 2010; Johnson, Onwuegbuzie, & Turner, 2007). By "rigorous," we mean data collection and analysis that is thorough and based on a predetermined and tested system. By "epistemologically sound," we mean data collection and analysis that is framed in a way that helps determine how we gain knowledge of what we know. Second, it involves the integration of qualitative and quantitative data in ways that underscore the advantages of using both research approaches to illuminate and advance our understanding of the phenomenon of interest. Sometimes it is difficult to locate true methods integration. However, all mixed methods studies, by definition, *imply* some form of integration of the data (Bazeley, 2009; Creswell & Plano, 2011); although the type and level of integration are subject to some continuing controversy (Creswell & Tashakkori, 2007). The premise and promise of integration of some aspect of qualitative and quantitative data is a guiding notion for us throughout the text as we describe (and then present) social work exemplars of mixed methods research. Integration is a benchmark of sorts and a question to pursue when complications arise in defining this continually developing area of research.

The definition of *mixed methods* is varied and evolving, and many scholars have weighed in with their descriptions, some of which we review here. Johnson and colleagues (2007) argue that mixed methods is one of three major research paradigms (i.e., qualitative research, quantitative research, and mixed methods research). The authors provide a consensus definition of *mixed methods*, as put forth by 21 researchers (none of whom were social workers), and then offer their own definition:

Mixed methods research is the type of research in which a researcher or a team of researchers combines elements of qualitative and quantitative research approaches (e.g. use of qualitative and quantitative viewpoints, data collection, analysis, inference techniques) for the broad purposes of breadth and depth of understanding and corroboration. (p. 123)

The definition of mixed methods as a methodology goes to another level and assumes that the methods cannot be separated from the research process itself, and therefore the definition proposed is very broad. It encompasses both inductive and deductive reasoning and adopts an underlying assumption that no research question can be adequately answered by a single method (or mono-method; Creswell & Tashakkori, 2007). Along this line, Creswell (2015) probably provides the most succinct definition of mixed methods research to date. He suggests that mixed methods is

an approach to research in the social, behavioral, and health sciences in which the investigator gathers both quantitative (closed-ended) and qualitative (open-ended) data, integrates the two, and then draws interpretations based on the combined strengths of both sets of data to understand research problems. (p. 2)

As a philosophical underpinning, Creswell (2015) looks at methods versus methodology (which would assume a mixing of paradigms) in his definition because this is the area of greatest growth. Methodologies are part researcher perspective and part philosophical worldview. It is how we determine everything about a study—how to frame the question, how to choose the sample, and what we anticipate learning from the individuals we have chosen to study. The methods are the tools and the ideas about how to go about answering our research question (Greene, 2007; Hesse-Biber, 2010). Researchers cannot really move into their area of inquiry unless they have taken an honest look at themselves and acknowledged their understanding of knowledge production and truth. Mertens (2010) also underscores the importance of philosophy in research and teaching mixed methods, as she affirms that we have a responsibility to encourage our students to make decisions about their methodological choices based on their philosophical assumptions.

Given the contributions of various disciplines in helping to shape what we know about mixed methods, we find it useful to acknowledge these disciplines in the definition of mixed methods. Though, we understand that this approach to defining mixed methods is not without its flaws. For example, Ivankova and Kawamura (2010) found that the identification of mixed methods studies in general is not easy for a number of reasons. In their review of mixed methods studies, they found that disciplines with the highest number of easily identified mixed methods studies (usually noted in the title or keywords) were health and medicine followed by education. But even in the studies where mixed methods techniques were included in the analysis, none seemed to have an overarching mixed methods question to guide the full study, and few provided meaningful integrated results (Ivankova & Kawamura, 2010). In social work, a mixed methods approach was predominantly found in evaluation studies, and the researchers mainly used a form of sequential design (described in more detail in chapter 2).

In public health, the literature on mixed methods highlights its benefits and challenges for investigating health disparities while offering exemplar studies after which future studies can be modeled (Stewart, Makwarimba, Barnfather, Letourneau, & Neufeld, 2008). In nursing, mixed methods research involves unpacking (or "unmixing") the quantitative and qualitative aspects of mixed methods to acquire a deeper understanding of what each paradigm contributes to solving problems (Sandelowski, 2014). In educational psychology, mixed methods is a methodology by which broad philosophies originate and that helps ascertain understanding of phenomena by way of interpretation and dissemination (Creswell, 2015; Creswell & Plano Clark, 2011). Despite the development of mixed methods in other disciplines, however, it is still a relatively new and underdeveloped way of thinking in social work.

THE DEFINITION OF MIXED METHODS IN SOCIAL WORK

We contend that mixed methods, as it is currently positioned in the social work profession, is all of the above: a paradigm, a methodology, and a philosophical underpinning. This is because mixed methods (much like social work) is rooted in pragmatism. Pragmatism as a worldview focuses on the consequences of research, on the primary importance of the question asked, and on the use of multiple methods of data collection to inform the problems under study. With mixed methods research in social work, data is collected and analyzed using both the deductive, or "top-down," quantitative approach, as well as the inductive, or "bottom-up," qualitative approach. Readers may recall from previous research methods courses that the top-down approach works from theory-to-hypothesis-to-data to confirm or contradict the theory. The bottom-up approach uses respondents' views to build broader themes and generate a theory interconnecting the themes.

Social work, for the most part, seems to have conformed to the general norms of mixed methods strategies developed by other health and social sciences researchers, adopting the mixed methods techniques of such disciplines as sociology (Small, 2011), public health (Curry & Nunez-Smith, 2015; Stewart et al., 2008), and nursing (Sandelowski, 2014). However, given the unique features of social work research and practice (and its contributions to marginalized individuals and communities), it seems appropriate for social work to carve out a distinctive mixed methods niche for its own researchers. Disaggregating the techniques of other disciplines and aggregating them into a guide that is practical—and specific—to the social work profession is one goal of this text. Similarly, we hope to answer some questions along the way about what mixed methods standards appear to be common across all disciplines and where we may need to cultivate strategies that adhere more closely to social work research norms and values. The mission of this book is to underscore the practicality, advantages, and value of using mixed methods to solve the problems traditionally found in social work.

There are advantages to using mixed methods in social work research. For example, Menon and Cowger (2010) outlined three advantages of integrating qualitative and quantitative methods in social work research. The authors suggested that integration "(a) proffers increased validity due to the triangulation of methods, (b) provides an opportunity to take advantage of the strengths of each approach, and (c) allows congruence with the principles of social work to study things holistically" (p. 612). Likewise, the use of mixed methods in social work research "improve[s] lives for individuals, groups, families, organizations, and communities; and make[s] the world a more just place for all" (Bronstein & Kovacs, 2013, p. 359). Although using mixed methods in social work can result in positive client outcomes, there are still some hurdles to overcome to maximize our use of mixed methods in social work.

In the health and social sciences, there have been debates about the most effective (or "correct") way to "do" mixed methods. Such discussions and debates in mixed methods research can be found in journal articles, books, and conference presentations, but a relatively small percentage of that discussion is specific to social work research. Ivankova and Kawamura (2010) were interested in looking at trends for what they call "integrated designs" in their chapter in the handbook *Mixed Methods in Social & Behavioral Research*. The authors tracked publications in health and medicine, social work, psychology, and other diverse areas like library science and engineering over a period of nine years (2000–2009). What they noticed first was that there was an increase in the number of publications claiming to use mixed methods designs. The reason most often given for choosing this integrative approach was that since the problems that were being investigated were complex, mixed methods designs were the most practical way to capture the necessary data. In a table comparing disciplines on their mixed methods empirical studies, social work research was late to the discussion and did not register any mixed methods articles until 2005, and then only had 27 listed by 2009 (Ivankova & Kawamura, 2010, p. 593). While not as rigorous in scope, a search of the term *mixed method* in the social work abstracts database yielded 90 articles published from 2010 to 2013. Although some of them were not written by social workers and a few were on specific data analysis methods, it seems clear that publications of mixed methods research studies in social work are increasing.

Mixed methods in social work research is also beginning to gain momentum at the conference level, as more studies using mixed methods are beginning to have a presence at the Society for Social Work Research (SSWR) Conference. In our review of SSWR presentations between 2009 and 2014, we found that a total of 19 presentations had the words "mixed methods" in the title. These presentations included papers, posters, symposiums, and workshops. One SSWR special interest group on mixed methods research was led by Deborah Gioia in 2011. Also noteworthy is the gradual increase (with a moderate decrease) of SSWR presentations with "mixed methods" in the title, as we found one presentation each during the 2009 and 2010 conferences, then three in 2011, six in 2012, and four each in 2013 and 2014. This growth is evident that we, as a profession, are beginning to think more about the ways in which we can use mixed methods not only in our social work practice but also our research. Given this, and for the purposes of this text, we propose our own definition of mixed methods in social work research:

> Mixed methods in social work research is the rigorous and epistemological application and integration of qualitative and quantitative research approaches to draw interpretations based on the combined strengths of both approaches for the purpose of influencing social work research, practice, and policy.

We have a few questions we hope to answer in this text: What is mixed methods? How does one "do" mixed methods? What does data integration look like? How are the methods prioritized? Is there evidence of a meaningful form of integration being achieved with our analytic processes, and how do we assess this integration? And finally, as social work researchers, how should we proceed with designing and conducting mixed methods? Should we work alone or with a team? Should we consider working with colleagues outside of our discipline? Before addressing these questions, we first remind readers of the purpose of this text and how it is organized and positioned in the social work profession.

This text reviews the fundamentals of mixed methods research designs, critically examines mixed method studies and models that have already been employed in social work, and considers the application of mixed methods research in social work settings. The text was written as a practical guide for conducting mixed methods research in social work settings. As such, the flow of the text is meant to use nine steps (and six "floors") to "walk" readers through how to do mixed methods research. Chapters 1, 5, and 6 provide supplemental material meant to serve as grounding for chapters 2, 3, and 4, which outline nine steps in the mixed methods research process specific to social work research.

Chapter 1 has provided an introduction to mixed methods. Chapter 2 begins by walking readers through (or "up") the figurative mixed methods "staircase" by first outlining how to design mixed methods studies in social work. Chapter 2 is divided into the first three steps of the mixed methods research process: (1) developing mixed methods purpose statements and research questions, (2) understanding mixed

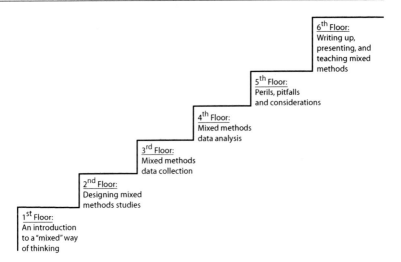

Figure 1.2. The six floors (chapters) for mixed methods research in this text.

methods design notation and language, and (3) choosing a mixed methods design. When readers reach the third floor (i.e., chapter 3), they will be ready to learn about mixed methods data collection in Steps 4, 5, and 6 of the mixed methods research process: (4) deciding on the data collection methods, (5) developing a sampling plan and recruitment strategies, and (6) collecting the data. By the time readers reach the fourth floor (i.e., chapter 4), they will be ready to cover the final steps in the mixed methods research process that involves the data analysis and the interpretation of findings. Thus chapter 4 is divided into the final three steps: (7) preparing the data for analysis, (8) analyzing the data, and (9) interpreting and presenting findings.

Chapter 5 presents the perils, pitfalls, and additional considerations of mixed methods research that are germane to social workers, as well as some exemplar mixed methods studies. We conclude our text with important elements involved in writing up, presenting, and teaching mixed methods in chapter 6. Figure 1.2 illustrates how this text is outlined.

2

"Second Floor": Designing Mixed Methods Studies

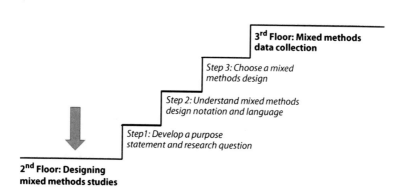

3rd Floor: Mixed methods data collection

Step 3: Choose a mixed methods design

Step 2: Understand mixed methods design notation and language

Step1: Develop a purpose statement and research question

2nd Floor: Designing mixed methods studies

This chapter covers the first three steps in our nine-step process for conducting mixed methods research in social work. First we discuss developing a purpose statement and research questions. Next we discuss mixed method design notation and language. Finally we share some popular mixed methods research designs overall, as well as those that are specific to social work, and the steps involved in actually choosing a mixed methods design. We begin this chapter with guidelines for developing a purpose statement and constructing research questions because we are operating under the assumption that social work researchers who have an interest in mixed methods research have already completed other very important steps in the research process, such as identifying the problem, reviewing the literature, assembling a team, and so on. We do not cover these steps of the research process here but encourage readers to visit other social work research and evaluation texts where these steps are presented (Grinnell & Unrau, 2014; Rubin & Babbie, 2013).

GETTING STARTED

At its foundation, a mixed methods design involves the inclusion of both qualitative and quantitative methods into a single study to generate a more comprehensive understanding of the phenomenon under study. Combining both qualitative and quantitative methods helps to expand the scope of the research. One advantage of mixed methods research is that it helps to maximize the strengths that each design brings to a project. Likewise, it offsets the weakness of each single method. Therefore, where each single method falls short, the other one helps to fill the gap to increase our understanding of the phenomenon of interest.

STEP 1:   DEVELOP A PURPOSE STATEMENT AND RESEARCH QUESTIONS

PURPOSE STATEMENTS

As social work researchers, it is fitting for us to acknowledge the importance of the purpose statement. To develop strong mixed methods purpose statements, it is helpful to first consider what strong qualitative and quantitative purpose statements look like. A strong qualitative purpose statement should include a central phenomenon and information about the participants, the research site, and the

Table 2.1. Characteristics of Qualitative and Quantitative Purpose Statements

Qualitative purpose statement includes	Quantitative purpose statement includes
• Central phenomenon	• Variables
• Participants	• Participants
• Research site	• Research site
• Qualitative design	• Quantitative method
• Action verbs	• Words that connect variables
• Nondirectional stance	• Directional language

qualitative design. Qualitative purpose statements also tend to include action verbs and take a nondirectional stance to a problem. Strong quantitative purpose statements include variables, as well as information about the participants, research site, and the quantitative method. They also include words that connect the variables and offer directional language. In Table 2.1, we provide some characteristics of qualitative and quantitative purpose statements.

A strong mixed methods purpose statement will include the overall intent of the study; phrases such as "the purpose of the study is . . ." are frequently used. A mixed methods purpose statement also includes the type of design that will be used in the mixed methods study, as well as a brief definition of the design, specific qualitative and quantitative purpose statements, and an explanation for why collecting qualitative and quantitative data may be necessary.

As described earlier, quantitative methods stem from a positivism worldview and seek to understand the breadth of the human experience. With quantitative methods, meaning is best acquired with numbers and counting things. Social workers are interested and highly invested in quantitative methods because of our interest in the number of peoples' lives that are affected by an experience or a certain phenomenon. However, quantitative methods are guided by quantitative research questions, whereas qualitative methods are guided by qualitative research questions. For instance, a *qualitative* research question might focus on participants' perceptions, impressions, or experiences of involvement in one group. However, a *quantitative* research question might compare outcomes on an intervention for two different groups.

RESEARCH QUESTIONS

Qualitative research questions are concise and open ended, and they tend to focus on one single concept. On the other hand, quantitative research may have either hypotheses or research questions (or both). Regardless, research questions and hypotheses relate variables between and across one another. Quantitative research questions and hypotheses are led by the literature. Also, compared to qualitative research questions, quantitative research questions and hypotheses can focus on multiple concepts (Table 2.2).

Qualitative and quantitative approaches to research have their own ways of framing the problem. We often note that qualitative questions tend to be framed as "why" and "how" questions, whereas quantitative questions tend to be framed as "what" and "how many" questions. We teach our students that when it comes to the relationship between qualitative and quantitative methods, qualitative research is the "voice" behind the "numbers" of quantitative research. Qualitative questions are framed as open-ended questions that help to capture the lived experiences of individuals and communities. Quantitative questions are framed in the form of testable hypotheses. With quantitative research, the goal is often to test for relationships between variables, with one or multiple independent variables and dependent variables. Most researchers find it helpful to have either hypotheses or research questions in their quantitative studies, although sometimes both can be used. The following are examples of a qualitative and a quantitative question.

(QUANT) Is there a statistically significant difference in social work student depressive symptoms as measure by the Beck Depression Inventory?

Table 2.2. The Difference Between Qualitative and Quantitative Research Questions

Qualitative research questions are	Quantitative research questions are
• Concise, simple • Open ended • Focused on a single concept	• Expansive, complex • Able to make predictions based on the literature • Focused on multiple concepts

(QUAL) What are the perceptions of social work students working with mentally ill clients during a clinical experience?

The distinction between what these two questions are measuring is clear: the quantitative research question focuses on obtaining statistical differences in Beck Depression Inventory scores, while the qualitative research question leads to a more in-depth description of the perceptions (maybe even the attitudes and beliefs) of social work students who work with mentally ill clients.

At this point in the research process, we always encourage social work researchers to *stop* and take a very close look at their purpose statement and research questions and decide if a mixed methods design is necessary. The reason for this is because we understand that with the popularity and allure of mixed methods research, it may seem like an obvious fit for social work research under every condition. However, its use may not always be necessary to answer one's research questions and accomplish one's research goals. As we alluded to earlier in the text, the type of method social workers select (i.e., quantitative, qualitative, or mixed method) should be a direct reflection of what they feel is the most appropriate way to answer their research questions, what matches their training or potential training, and what is aligned with their worldview.

MIXED METHODS RESEARCH QUESTIONS

Overall, strong research questions in mixed methods studies usually address the mixing of the two single-method phases; they can be predetermined or emergent, independent or dependent, and written in different forms. They can be written as a question, a hypothesis, or a study aim. In some instances a mixed methods research question can include a separate quantitative and qualitative question if both narrative and numerical data are desired. Despite the growing mixed methods literature, sources suggest there is a dearth of resources that offer guidance on *how* to write mixed methods research questions. Although social workers may have a sense for the types of mixed methods research questions they want to ask, they must be deliberate about their understanding of what each method can bring to the table and how each method—individually, then paired with the other—can address the overall research question. Hesse-Biber (2010) suggests that several factors may influence a researcher's decisions when constructing a mixed methods research question: the serendipity factor, the iterative factor, and the researcher's standpoint. The moment when the language used to ask the question shifts from "how" to "what" and, alternatively, from "what" to "how," is when the mixing of methods emerges. A methodological shift occurs—thereby the researcher's standpoint also shifts (Hesse-Biber, 2010). When developing a mixed methods research question, keep in mind the various complexities of developing research questions more broadly. For example, Hesse-Biber offers some criteria for assessing the various facets of a research question. She suggests researchers pose a series of questions to themselves and members of their team, such as:

- Is your question feasible? Can you research this question? Do you have time, money, and research skills to proceed to answer this question?
- Is the question ethical—that is, does it meet the standards of an institutional review board (IRB) ethics evaluation?
- Is the problem stated in a way that addresses the variety of different concerns/issues surrounding a given research problem?
- Is the research problem clearly stated and focused? Did the researcher define his or her main concepts?
- Is your question significant? There are a number of ways in which a research problem might be considered significant: Does the research problem add value to the existing literature? Does it suggest a new area for inquiry that looks promising? Does the research problem address an important research area in need of new knowledge? (p. 49)

The best way to really understand how mixed methods research questions can be constructed is to see an example. Table 2.3 demonstrates what both quantitative and qualitative methods can contribute to addressing a social work problem. In this example, which focuses on health literacy and prenatal services for low-income mothers, we also provide suggestions for ways to address the problem using both qualitative and quantitative methods.

Table 2.3. Using Quantitative and Qualitative Methods to Answer a Social Work Problem

Social Work Problem: Health literacy concerns in the delivery of prenatal services to low-income mothers by OB/GYNs at a health clinic

Mixed Methods Research Question: How do the health literacy perspectives of pregnant, low-income mothers compare to survey data collected from the OB/GYNs who deliver prenatal services to them?

Qualitative methods	*Quantitative methods*
• Focus groups can be conducted with the mothers to determine their prenatal service needs. • One-on-one interviews can be conducted (during the lunch hour) with OB/GYNs to understand their service goals during encounters with pregnant, low-income mothers, their prenatal education, and behaviors. • Appointments between the mothers and their OB/GYN can be observed for deeper understanding of each one's comfort with discussing prenatal services.	• Satisfaction surveys (paper copies) can be completed by pregnant, low-income mothers in the waiting room to rate their level of satisfaction with and understanding of the current services being offered. • E-mail surveys can be completed by OB/GYNs to ascertain their expectations for and comfort with working with low-income mothers, cultural sensitivity, and communication strategies. • The mothers' patient records can be used to acquire information about potential challenges to their understanding and/or receptivity of prenatal education delivered by their OB/GYNs.

While both methods are valuable, the two different types of data offer two different ways of addressing the research question. Consider another example involving a substance-abuse intervention that includes both men and women. A quantitative method might assess gender differences in the intervention outcomes (i.e., compare intervention outcomes of men to those of women). However, a qualitative method might include a deeper probing into the outcomes, as it will also be able to capture specific language from both male and female participants regarding their perceptions, impressions, and experiences with services while participating in the substance-abuse intervention.

Next, we want to underscore an important (yet often overlooked) aspect of mixed methods research questions. That is, that mixed methods research questions can be written in different ways. Earlier we described the characteristics of an ideal mixed methods research question. Yet, how a mixed methods research question is written is what truly distinguishes a "good" one from a bad one. Some researchers write their research questions so that they are "method" focused; an example is "To what extent do the qualitative results confirm the quantitative results?" Other researchers may decide to write questions that are more "content" (or topic) focused. An example of a content-focused question is "How do the perspectives of adolescent boys support the results that their self-esteem changes during the middle school years?" But an ideal mixed methods research question is one that includes a little of both: the method and the content (one that is both method focused and content focused). An example of such an ideal research question is "What results emerge from comparing the exploratory qualitative data about boys' self-esteem with quantitative outcome data measured using a self-esteem instrument?" By mentioning the part about comparing the exploratory qualitative data to the quantitative outcome data, the method requirements are met. Likewise, by mentioning boys' self-esteem, the content (i.e., topic) requirement of the mixed methods study is addressed. We elaborate on mixed methods research questions in Step 3 of our nine steps of mixed methods research in social work.

STEP 2:   UNDERSTAND MIXED METHODS DESIGN NOTATION AND LANGUAGE

Janice Morse (1991) was the first to conceptualize a notation system, which helped to formalize mixed methods as an approach with its own standards, procedures, and notations. In Table 2.4, we illustrate our adapted version of this notation system, complete with examples and a key to help readers understand what the notation system means. The shorthand for quantitative data is "quan," and the shorthand for qualitative data is "qual." Uppercase QUAN and QUAL are usually used to indicate which data is treated as the priority in a study; likewise, lowercase "quan" and "qual" are used to indicate which data are treated as secondary, or as a supplement to the priority data. The plus sign (+) is used to demonstrate that the quantitative and qualitative methods occur simultaneously or concurrently, and the arrow (→) suggests that the methods occur sequentially. Parentheses are used to indicate that one method

Table 2.4. Notations Commonly Used in Mixed Methods Research Designs

Depiction	Design notation	Example of use	Definition
Shorthand	Quan, Qual	"The Qual strand of the study involves focus groups."	Shorthand way to write "quantitative" and "qualitative"
Uppercase	QUAN, QUAL	"The QUAL methods were completed first."	Whichever methods are capitalized are prioritized in the mixed methods design
Lowercase	quan, qual	"We used the qual method to supplement the QUAN method."	Whichever methods are lowercased have a lesser priority in the mixed methods design
Plus sign	+	"We implemented a QUAN + qual design"	The QUAN and qualitative methods occur concurrently, but the QUAN is prioritized
Arrow	→	"We implemented a QUAN → qual design"	The methods occur in a sequence whereby the QUAN methods are followed by qual methods
Parentheses	( )	"QUAN (qual)"	The method in the parentheses is embedded within a larger design (or procedure) or mixed within a theoretical framework
Brackets	[ ]	qual → QUAN → [QUAN + qual]	A mixed methods design is embedded in another. The [QUAN + qual] is used within a single study or within a series of studies

is embedded within another method or that a procedure is mixed within a theoretical or program-objective framework. Brackets ([ ]) are often used when a mixed methods project is implemented within a single study or within a series of studies.

Beyond the mixed methods design notation and language, one must understand how the two data phases are connected. Although we expound on the actual "mixing" of mixed methods in chapter 4, we provide a brief description of the ways that data are mixed here to help readers with their understanding of mixed methods design notation and language. In mixed methods research, the methods can be mixed in a few ways. Some of the more popular ways are by merging the data, connecting the data, or embedding the data. *Merging the data* consists of combining the qualitative data (in text or images) with the quantitative data (in numeric form). An example of this is showing differences among the qualitative categories and quantitative ratings in a table format. *Connecting the data* involves analyzing one type of data then using the information to inform the subsequent data collection. This connects the analysis of results from phase 1 of a project (the first method) with the data collection of phase 2 (the second method). Thus the mixing is sequential in nature. *Embedding the data* is when a data set of second priority is embedded within a larger, primary mixed methods design. For example, the qualitative data of a study can sometimes help explain the quantitative data or vice versa. Regardless of how the data are mixed, mixed methods research involves combining qualitative and quantitative data within the context of a single research study. The goal of mixed methods research is not to replace either of these approaches but rather to draw from the strengths and minimize the weaknesses of both in single research studies or across studies.

Strong mixed methods studies must employ a framework to assess the quality in the data from both single-method approaches, the interpretation, and the rigor. Frameworks put forward by O'Cathain (2010) and Nastasi, Hitchcock, and Brown (2010) are useful templates to consult when designing a mixed methods study in order to interrogate all facets of the research effort. O'Cathain offers readers a framework for judging mixed methods studies, while in their chapter from the same volume, Nastasi et al. provide a critical review of various mixed methods designs.

STEP 3: CHOOSE A MIXED METHODS DESIGN

After social work researchers have determined the purpose statement, drafted the research questions, and gained a good understanding of mixed methods design and notation, they should choose a mixed methods design to use for their study. In this section, we begin with general considerations for choosing a mixed methods design. Then we present the six most popular designs: the convergent parallel design, the explanatory sequential design, the exploratory sequential design, the embedded design, the transformative design, and the multiphase design (Creswell, 2015; Creswell & Plano Clark, 2011). We conclude with key decisions that must be made when choosing a mixed methods design.

GENERAL CONSIDERATIONS FOR HOW TO CHOOSE A MIXED METHODS DESIGN

At its core, mixed methods research is used for exploring the meaning of a construct or phenomenon from more than one perspective. But it is important to understand that some specific questions call for mixed methods research. For example, mixed methods research is needed for explaining the anomalous findings of getting to the bottom of a mechanism of action or an effect. Mixed methods research can also be used for testing or extending a theory or for developing a measure using grounded theory approaches. Finally, mixed methods research can be used for augmenting evaluation studies with a better understanding for how the intervention was implemented.

When designing a mixed methods study, researchers have several characteristics to consider. For example, the design can be *fixed* or *emergent*. A fixed design might be needed when the sample is discrete and can be specified—even for the qualitative sample (i.e., classroom, hospital unit). Also, researchers must identify an approach to the design, based on the research question. Designs can be matched to the research problem, purpose, and/or question. Note that emergent designs do not indicate poor planning by the researcher; rather they imply that data analysis is ongoing and will necessitate changes to multiple parts of the study design as one begins data collection (Creswell & Plano Clark, 2011). Regardless of which design is selected, researchers should be able to clearly articulate their reasons for mixing the methods, as this will help to strengthen the credibility of the study.

When choosing a mixed methods design, certain aspects of the study should be taken into consideration. First, the design should be considered in the context of the qualitative phase (also called "strand" by some mixed methods scholars), as well as the quantitative phase of the study.

In other words, the chosen design should be one that allows research-ers to maximize their use of both the qualitative and the quantitative phases of the mixed methods study. Next, there should be sufficient bal-ance between the saturation of the phenomenon and the representative-ness of the examination. Other things to consider are that one sample may be a subset of the other sample. For example, perhaps the qualitative sample used can be taken from the larger, quantitative sample. Decisions such as these should be made at the beginning of a mixed methods study. However, these decisions are often modified as the study progresses. Another consideration to make when designing mixed methods studies is whether both studies should use the same total sample. This is likely to occur. Sequential mixed methods sampling can occur, whereby the sample information from the first method is used to draw a sample for the second method (Creswell & Plano Clark, 2011). Based on the nature of the study, there may also be an opportunity to apply a mixed methods sampling strategy, which involves using probability and purposive sam-pling techniques at different levels of analysis. An example of this type of study is one that includes different types of research participants, such as a hospital-based study that includes both clinicians and patients/clients.

MIXED METHODS DESIGNS

We have already discussed some basic characteristics of mixed methods research designs. Next we discuss some of the more popular designs in the mixed methods literature. The six mixed methods research designs that appear most widely in the literature are the convergent parallel design, the explanatory sequential design, the exploratory sequential design, the embedded design, the transformative design, and the multi-phase design. We describe each of these below.

Convergent Parallel Design

One of the most popular mixed methods designs is the convergent par-allel design. When using the convergent parallel design, the researcher collects quantitative and qualitative data concurrently, analyzes the two data sets separately, and then mixes the qualitative and quantitative data phases by merging the results during interpretation (and sometimes during data analysis). As for the philosophical assumptions through which the convergent parallel design is best received, an "umbrella" paradigm and worldview is typically used. An example of such a worldview is pragmatism, since it embraces mixed methods. Other names for the convergent parallel design include parallel-databases variant, data-transformation variant, and data-validation variant (Creswell & Plano Clark, 2011). A social worker will often select a convergent parallel design when he or she needs to obtain a more complete understanding from the qualitative and quantitative data, plans to corroborate results from different methods, or wants to compare multiple levels within a system. Researchers who consider using the convergent parallel design usually do so if they need to collect both types of data in one visit to the field, if both types of data have equal value for understanding the research problem, if the researchers have quantitative and qualitative research skills, and/or if they can manage extensive data collection activities individually or with a team. A convergent parallel design is depicted in Figure 2.1.

The convergent parallel design has a number of strengths that make it an attractive choice for social work researchers interested in mixed methods research. First, this design is intuitive. Researchers who are new to mixed methods often choose this design because of the clear distinction between the qualitative and quantitative methods and the convenience of not needing to relate the findings from the two phases until the analysis and/or interpretation phase of the study. Next, the convergent parallel design is efficient. Both types of data are collected during one phase of the study, which saves time. Finally, the convergent parallel

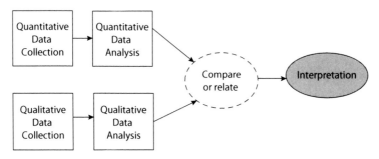

Figure 2.1. Convergent parallel design.

design is team-friendly. Each phase can be collected and analyzed separately, using techniques that are germane to each data type. This lends itself to team research, in which the team can include individuals who are proficient with either qualitative or quantitative research.

Some challenges with the convergent parallel design are that it requires substantial effort and expertise. Also, researchers must deal with issues related to the differing samples and sample sizes. Some researchers also find it challenging to merge two sets of very different data and their results in a meaningful way. Though, a way to address this concern is to be sure that the design of the qualitative and quantitative studies addresses the same concepts. Researchers may face the question of what to do if the quantitative and qualitative results do not agree. This is not always a disadvantage and, in fact, is often considered a strength of mixed methods studies. Contradictions may provide new insight on the topic, but these differences can be difficult to resolve and may require the collection of additional data. The question then develops into what type of additional data needs to be collected or reanalyzed: quantitative data, qualitative data, or both? Thus the convergent parallel design can be a good design for a social worker conducting a mixed methods study for the first time.

Explanatory Sequential Design

When using the explanatory sequential design, researchers begin by collecting and analyzing quantitative data, then they collect and analyze qualitative data in a second phase (as a follow-up to the quantitative results). For an explanatory sequential design, the quantitative results shape the qualitative research questions, sampling, and data collection. The explanatory sequential design gets its name from the explanatory nature of quantitative data. Thinking back to the knowledge-level continuum referenced earlier in the text, you will recall that quantitative data helps to achieve explanation and relationships between variables (Grinnell & Unrau, 2014). Since the quantitative phase occurs prior to the qualitative phase, this design is called the explanatory sequential design.

With the explanatory sequential design, everything begins with a quantitative phase. Therefore, the research problem and purpose often call for greater emphasis to be placed on the quantitative features of the study. Because of this, researchers may find themselves using a positivist approach to the study (i.e., subjective and objective inquiry are valued but objective context is needed for the experiment). Despite this, it is recommended that researchers consider using different assumptions with each phase. In other words, since the study begins with a quantitative phase, researchers should begin from the perspective of positivism to develop instruments, measure variables, and assess statistical results. When researchers move to the qualitative phase that values multiple perspectives and in-depth descriptions, they should consider the assumptions of constructivism (i.e., subjective inquiry with multiple realities). Thus the overall philosophical assumptions for an explanatory sequential design would shift halfway through the study. The purpose of the explanatory sequential design is to use qualitative data to help explain quantitative results that need further exploration and to use quantitative results to purposefully select the best direction for a qualitative study. Some scholars argue that this design is the most straightforward of all the mixed methods research designs. Figure 2.2 provides a visual depiction of the explanatory sequential design. As pictured, researchers move from quantitative data collection and analysis to results, which they then follow up with qualitative data collection and analysis. The overall interpretation occurs at the end of the study.

Despite its popularity, the explanatory sequential design should be used only under certain conditions. For example, this design should be considered if the research problem is quantitatively oriented; that way, the primary focus of the study can be conducted at the front end of the project. Also, an explanatory sequential design may be used if the social

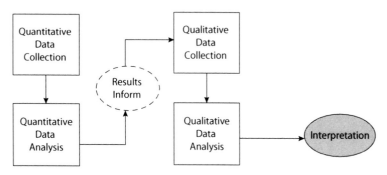

Figure 2.2. Explanatory sequential design.

work researcher is quantitatively oriented. If the researcher knows important variables and instruments are available, he or she may also decide to use an explanatory sequential design over another design. This is because the variables can be tested (and instruments disseminated) in the first phase of the study; then the qualitative data can be used to confirm, complement, or explain the first quantitative phase. Another condition under which the explanatory sequential design may be selected is if researchers have limited resources and need to collect and analyze one data type at a time. Finally, if researchers anticipate that new questions may emerge from quantitative results, they may opt for an explanatory sequential design.

Some strengths of the explanatory sequential design include its appeal to pure quantitative researchers and its straightforward and self-contained framework that includes the completion of one phase first, then completion of the next phase. Also, teams who feel a sense of urgency to disseminate study findings will find that the explanatory sequential design allows for the ease of writing the final report as two separate phases, which may be attractive to teams that include pure quantitative and qualitative experts. This design also provides an opportunity to explore, qualitatively, a concept that emerges from the quantitative data. Despite the benefits, challenges also exist with the explanatory sequential design. For example, oftentimes two phases require a long time to implement, and it can be difficult to secure IRB approval when the second phase cannot be specified before the first phase is complete. Also, social work researchers must decide what quantitative results to follow up with and the criteria for selecting participants, and it can sometimes be challenging to contact participants for a second round of data collection. If quantitative data is not a priority, the exploratory sequential design may be preferred.

Exploratory Sequential Design

With the exploratory sequential design, researchers collect qualitative data then analyze the qualitative data and use its results to build on a subsequent quantitative phase. Data phases of the exploratory sequential design are connected when the qualitative results are used to shape the quantitative phase by specifying research questions and variables, developing an instrument, and/or generating a typology

(Creswell & Plano Clark, 2011). When thinking about the exploratory nature of qualitative research (i.e., the knowledge-level continuum), it is easy to see why the qualitative phase occurs first in the exploratory sequential design. With the exploratory sequential design, researchers begin with constructivism (because the qualitative phase occurs first) then shift to positivism to accommodate the quantitative phase of the study. Also, in this design the qualitative phase has greater priority than the quantitative phase. Other names for this design include the theory-development design and the instrument-development design.

The purpose of the exploratory sequential design is to explore concepts related to the phenomenon of interest because variables, theories, and hypotheses are not known. Another purpose is to develop an instrument or typology that is not available and/or to assess whether qualitative themes can be used to develop a quantitative dataset that can be generalized to a population. Figure 2.3 illustrates the exploratory sequential design. Researchers using the exploratory sequential design begin with a qualitative phase that includes data collection and analyses. In the next step, which is the point of interface in the data mixing, the researchers use results from the qualitative phase to develop an instrument, identify variables, or state propositions for testing based on an emergent theory or framework.

Much like the other designs, exploratory sequential designs should be selected by social work researchers only under certain conditions. These conditions include when the researcher and research problem are qualitatively oriented, when important variables are not known and instruments are not available, when the researcher has time to conduct

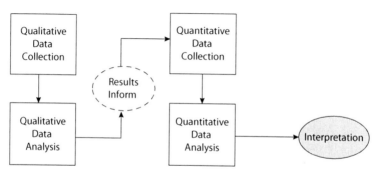

Figure 2.3. Exploratory sequential design.

two phases, when the researcher has limited resources and needs to collect and analyze one data type at a time, and when new questions have
emerged from qualitative results. Strengths of the exploratory sequential design include the fact that it is fairly straightforward to design,
implement, and report. It also has a quantitative component that can
make the qualitative approach more acceptable to quantitative-biased
audiences. For example, the researcher produces a quantitative-oriented
product, such as an instrument.

Social work researchers often find that the exploratory sequential
design lends itself to emergent approaches. Despite the strengths, however, there are also some challenges to the exploratory sequential design.
For example, it has two phases, which means that it may require a lot of
time to implement, especially if the qualitative phase is ethnographic
in nature or saturation of the qualitative findings is difficult to ascertain. Also, there are often difficulties specifying the quantitative procedures when applying for initial IRB approval. Therefore researchers may
need to consider submitting an amendment that outlines the emergent
nature of the study. Deciding which of the qualitative findings to use for
the quantitative phase can also be challenging, as well as following the
appropriate procedures for developing a valid and reliable instrument.
Creswell (2015) states that the convergent, explanatory sequential, and
exploratory sequential designs are all "basic" designs and that any one
of these designs is really the foundation of every mixed methods study.
The next three designs we discuss (according to Creswell and others) are
more "advanced" because they extend the conceptualization and implementation of the basic designs.

Embedded Design

When considering an embedded design, researchers must decide that
they want to collect and analyze additional quantitative and qualitative data within a quantitative research study or a qualitative research
study or procedure. Researchers then collect and analyze this second
set of data. This can occur before, during, and/or after the collection
and analysis of the first set of data. The purpose of the embedded design
is to address different questions that call for different methods or to
enhance an experiment. This enhancement often involves improving
recruitment procedures, examining the intervention process, and/or

explaining reactions to participation. The philosophical assumptions for the embedded design are established by the primary approach, and thus the other data is subservient within that method. For example, if the primary design is experimental, correlational, longitudinal, or focused on instrument validation, then the researcher will most likely be working from positivist assumptions as the overarching paradigm. Likewise, if the primary design is phenomenological, grounded theory, ethnographical, or narrative, the researcher will likely be working from a constructivist paradigm (Creswell & Plano Clark, 2011). With both cases, the supplemental method has a supporting role. An example of an embedded design can be viewed in Figure 2.4.

In this example, the qualitative data collection and analysis can be embedded within a primary quantitative (or qualitative) study design. The timing of the embedded phase can be before, during, or after the primary phase of the study. The decision around the timing of the embedded phase is based on the purpose of the supplemental data within the larger design. Procedures for an embedded design may include designing the overall experiment and determining why qualitative (or quantitative) data need to be included, collecting and analyzing qualitative data to enhance the experimental design, collecting and analyzing quantitative outcome data for the experimental groups, and interpreting how the qualitative results enhance the experimental procedures and/or understanding of the experimental outcomes (Creswell & Plano Clark, 2011).

Researchers often choose the embedded design if they have expertise with the primary design, are comfortable with the primary orientation, and have little prior experience with the supplemental (second) method.

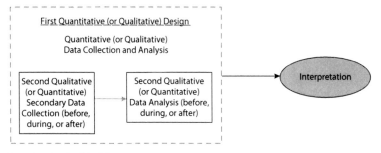

Figure 2.4. Embedded design.

The embedded design may also be selected if the resources limit placing equal priority on both methods; and/or if there is a need for the supplemental method and the data that emerges from it. Strengths of the embedded design are that it may require less time and fewer resources, especially if resources from the primary method can be used to collect data for the supplemental method. Also, the embedded design may improve the larger design with supplemental data, and it often fits the social work research team approach very well. Challenges with the embedded design are that social workers may need expertise in the primary method used and the purpose and the timing of the supplemental data collection must be specified. Also, results for the embedded design are sometimes difficult to integrate, as the supplemental data may be mistakenly treated as tangential data unrelated to the project rather than supplemental data that will enhance the study findings. Given the nature of social work research and practice, we assume that the embedded design will be of particular interest given its intervention focus. It may seem to be a natural extension (or next step) for many social workers interested in mixed methods to simply embed another data phase within a current one. Although we believe that the embedded design is a natural extension of social work interventions, from a philosophical perspective we also believe that the transformative design will be of particular interest to social workers.

Transformative Design

The transformative design, because of its social justice undercurrents, seems like an appropriate design for social workers who are interested in mixed methods research. The transformative design may be called by other names, such as the feminist lens, disability lens, or socioeconomic class lens, which all have implications for social work research and practice (Creswell, 2015; Mertens, 2009). Using a transformative design means that the researcher is using a theoretical-based framework to advance the inquiry needs of underrepresented or marginalized populations. The researcher then collects and analyzes quantitative and qualitative data concurrently or sequentially. A philosophical assumption of this design is that the transformative paradigm (Mertens, 2009, 2013) provides the overarching assumptions behind the conduct of the transformative design. This worldview (which is also aligned with the advocacy and participatory worldview) provides an umbrella to the project and includes political action, empowerment, collaborative, and change-oriented research perspectives (Creswell & Plano Clark, 2011; Mertens, 2013). The purpose of the transformative design is to conduct research that is "change oriented" and seeks to advance social justice causes.

Given the description of the transformative design (and Figure 2.5), readers may have noticed something very familiar: it looks just like the explanatory sequential design. This is true. While the transformative mixed methods research design looks very similar to the explanatory sequential design, the difference is that the transformative paradigm and theoretical lens used by the researcher have pervasive influence throughout the entire research process. So, during each step, the transformative paradigm plays a role, and there is a consistent focus on social justice during each phase of this design.

Researchers may choose this design if they are seeking to address issues of social justice and call for change, want to focus on the needs of underrepresented or marginalized populations, have a good working knowledge of social justice theoretical frameworks, and can conduct the study without further marginalizing the population under study. Strengths of the transformative design are that it is positioned within a transformative framework; it helps to empower individuals and bring about change; participants often play a participatory role in the study; and it may produce results useful to community members and credible to stakeholders. On the other hand, challenges also exist. One of the biggest challenges of the transformative design is that social workers often have sparse peer-reviewed literature to support their work and provide guidance. Little guidance may often mean that the approach will need to be justified before use. The transformative design is one in which social workers must develop trust with the study participants and conduct research in a culturally sensitive way.

Another name for the transformative design, as conceptualized by other mixed methods scholars, is the social justice design, which (based on the title) underscores the mission and focus of social work. Also, this design presumes that any theoretical underpinning can be used as the lens through which the mixed methods work is completed. Figure 2.5 illustrates an example of a mixed methods design that incorporates a profeminist lens. Something else readers may have noticed by now is the

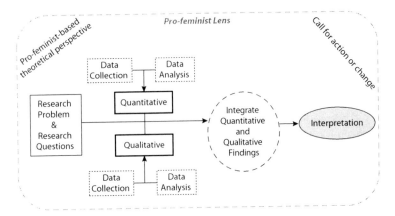

Figure 2.5. Transformative design.

transformative framework's close resemblance to participatory action research and/or community-based participatory research. As we were trained across multiple disciplines, our own transformative design work began to be reflective of other disciplines and raised the question: What is the difference between the transformative design and participatory action research and/or community-based participatory research? While we do not expound on this here, we posit that it seems as though the three are similar and complementary to one another. The characteristics of one are not perfectly mapped onto the other, yet the collaborative elements of participatory action research and community-based participatory research can be applied with transformation as a goal.

Multiphase Design

The purpose of the multiphase design is to address a set of incremental questions that advance one programmatic objective. When considering the multiphase design, researchers examine an overall objective, implement an iteration of connected quantitative and/or qualitative studies, and then build each new study on what was learned previously. In terms of philosophical assumptions with the multiphase design, these can vary depending on the specifics of the project. Experts suggest pragmatism be used as an umbrella foundation if phases are implemented concurrently and that constructivism be used for the qualitative component

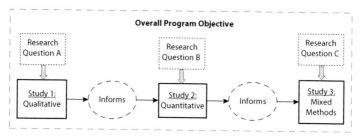

Overall Program Objective

Research Question A

Research Question B

Research Question C

Study 1: Qualitative

Informs

Study 2: Quantitative

Informs

Study 3: Mixed Methods

Figure 2.6. Multiphase design.

and positivism for the quantitative component if the phases are sequential (Creswell & Plano Clark, 2011). Figure 2.6 illustrates the multiphase design.

The multiphase design is structured so that each individual study addresses a specific set of research questions, which evolve to address a larger program objective. These procedures within a given study phase, or sequence of studies, may mirror the procedures for implementing one or more of the basic mixed methods designs. Creswell and Plano Clark (2011) suggest that researchers utilizing a multiphase design carefully state the research questions for each study, which both contribute to the overall program of inquiry and build on what has been acquired in previous phases, and design procedures that build on the earlier study findings.

Researchers may choose the multiphase design if they cannot fill a long-term objective with a single mixed methods study, have experience in large-scale or longitudinal research, have sufficient resources and funding, have a team that includes practitioners and researchers, and have emergent questions that arise at different stages. A strength of the multiphase design is that it is flexible, so it allows social workers to address interconnected questions. Also, social workers may find it rather easy to publish individual results while contributing to the larger program objective. Multiphase designs often fit well with program evaluation and development plans. Furthermore, they provide a framework for multiple studies over several years. Challenges with the multiphase design are that social work researchers must anticipate needing sufficient resources, time, and effort to complete their studies over time. This is despite the fact that there are often limitations in the amount of resources available to social services agencies to conduct such research. Multiphase designs mean that individuals are (or should be) effectively collaborating on a team (which may pose challenges, given the time, resources, and efforts of individuals and agencies). Also, it can be challenging to decide how to meaningfully connect individual studies. Social work researchers may find that they need to translate research into practice, which can be time-consuming and resource-intensive, especially if they are in an agency that values research. In addition, multiphase design studies may require multiple IRB applications or amendments before, during, and after implementation.

KEY DECISIONS IN CHOOSING A MIXED METHODS STUDY DESIGN

Some key decisions need to be made when choosing a mixed methods design. These decisions involve four major aspects of the study: (a) the mixed methods research question, (b) the level of interaction between the phases, (c) the priority of the phases, and (d) the timing of the phases. We discuss each of these next.

First, *the mixed methods research questions* can help solidify which type of mixed methods design to use. When the time comes to write research questions, it is almost second nature to think about how the questions can be influenced by the mixed methods design and vice versa. Some examples of research questions that are specific to a few popular mixed methods designs that we presented earlier are provided in Table 2.5.

The second aspect of the mixed methods study that influences the design is *the level of interaction between the qualitative and quantitative phases.* This is the extent to which the two phases are kept independent or interact with one another. An independent level of interaction occurs when the quantitative and qualitative phases are implemented so that each one is independent from the other—that is, the two phases are distinct and the researcher keeps the quantitative and qualitative research questions, data collection, and data analysis separate. When the level of interaction is independent, the researcher mixes the two phases only when drawing conclusions during the overall interpretation at the end of the study. An interactive level of interaction occurs when a direct interaction exists between the quantitative and qualitative phases of the study. Through this direct interaction, the two methods are mixed before the final interpretation. This interaction can occur at different

Table 2.5. Examples of Research Questions Specific to Mixed Methods Designs

Sample research question	Design
"To what extent do the quantitative and qualitative results converge?"	Convergent parallel design
"In what ways do the qualitative data help to explain the quantitative results?"	Explanatory sequential design
"In what ways do the quantitative results generalize the qualitative findings?"	Exploratory sequential design
"How do the qualitative findings provide a deeper understanding of the quantitative results?"	Embedded design
"How do the qualitative findings provide a deeper understanding of the quantitative results in order to explore service inequalities among our clients?"	Transformative design
"How do the qualitative findings provide a deeper understanding of the quantitative results in order to explore inequalities for this first phase of the intervention?"	Multiphase design

points in the research process and in many different ways. For example, the design and conduct of one phase of the study may depend on the results from the other phase. By way of illustration, the data from one phase (e.g., qualitative codes) may be converted into the other type of data (e.g., quantitative frequencies) and then the different data sets analyzed together, or one data point may be implemented within a framework based on the other data.

The third key decision when choosing a mixed methods study design is *the priority of the quantitative and qualitative phases.* "Priority" refers to the relative importance or weighting of the quantitative and qualitative methods for answering the study's questions. There are three possible weighting options: (a) the two methods may have equal priority so that both play an equally important role in addressing the research question; (b) the study may use a quantitative priority whereby a greater emphasis is placed on the quantitative methods and the qualitative methods are used in a secondary, more supplemental role; and (c) the study may use a qualitative priority where a greater emphasis is placed on the qualitative methods and the quantitative methods are used in a secondary, more supplemental role.

The *timing of the quantitative and qualitative phases* is the fourth key decision that needs to be made when choosing a mixed methods design. Timing (also referred to as "pacing" or "implementation") refers to the chronological relationship between the quantitative and qualitative phases within a mixed methods study. Timing is often discussed relative to the time the data are collected, but, more important, it describes the order in which researchers use the results from the two sets of data within a mixed methods study. Timing relates to the entire quantitative and qualitative processes of the mixed methods study (not just data collection within each phase) and it is classified in three ways: concurrent timing, sequential timing, and multiphase combination timing. Each has a distinct role and responsibility in a mixed methods study. *Concurrent timing* occurs when the researcher implements both the quantitative and the qualitative phases during a single phase of the study. *Sequential timing* occurs when the researcher implements the phases during two distinct time periods, with the collection and analysis of one type of data occurring after the collection and analysis of the other. A researcher using sequential timing may choose to start by either collecting and analyzing quantitative data first or collecting and analyzing qualitative data first. *Multiphase combination timing* occurs when the researcher implements multiple phases that include sequential and/or concurrent timing over an entire program of study. Examples of multiphase combination timing include studies conducted over three or more phases, as well as those that combine both concurrent and sequential elements within one mixed methods study.

STEPS IN CHOOSING A MIXED METHODS DESIGN

We understand that readers of this pocket guide to mixed methods research in social work want to gain some valuable (and concise) information about how to conduct mixed methods research. Given this, we suggest some specific steps that readers should follow when choosing a mixed methods design (also presented in Table 2.6). First, when choosing a mixed methods design we recommend researchers review (over and over again) the purpose of the study. This may involve reviewing the research questions for the study, and making edits to them, to ensure that they line up with the study goals. It is difficult to move

Table 2.6. Six Steps in Choosing a Mixed Methods Design

1. Review the purpose of the study.
2. Focus on the *intent* of the study (i.e., what it will accomplish).
3. Consider a "basic" design:
   a. Will it be a convergent, explanatory sequential, or exploratory sequential design?
   b. Will the data need to be merged during the study or connected at a later stage of the study?
4. Consider whether, based on the intent, features should be added that extend the basic design; that is, should it be a transformative study, an embedded study, or a multistage study?
5. Review current scientific literature to see which mixed methods designs have been used in the past.
6. Find colleagues who can assist with various stages of the design.

forward in a mixed method study (or any study for that matter) without a clear understanding for why the topic is being explored in the first place. Second, researchers should take into the consideration the *intent* of the study. The intent is similar to, but not the same as, the purpose. While the purpose of the study describes what the researcher hopes to do, the intent of the study is what the researcher hopes to accomplish, overall, by conducting the research. A large part of this second step is making sure that the study's purpose, research questions, goals, and intent are all aligned. In the third step for choosing a mixed method design, researchers should consider whether the research team will likely merge the data or connect it at a later stage of the study (Creswell, 2015). That way they will have some sense for whether the design should be convergent (merging the data) or sequential (connecting the data). Creswell would suggest (and we agree) that this is the step where the researcher determines his or her "basic" mixed methods design. In the fourth step for choosing a mixed methods design, researchers should revisit the intent of the study and decide if any additional features need to be included in the design. For example, as social workers, we tend to be involved in individual and community-level interventions. If the intent of the study is to improve the social conditions of a community of interest through the delivery of an intervention, chances are, this level of detail will need to be included in the mixed methods design. Also, because of their social justice worldview, social work researchers may decide to include a certain "lens" that is applied to every stage of the mixed methods process.

The fifth step for choosing a mixed methods research design includes reviewing peer-reviewed literature using scientific and academic databases (e.g., PsycINFO, EBSCOhost, ScienceDirect, Google Scholar) to see what other research designs have been used in similar studies. Keep in mind that the studies found in these scientific and academic databases may or may not use mixed methods approaches. Even if the studies use a single-method approach, the decisions that researchers made within those designs can help inform the decisions a researcher makes for the qualitative and/or quantitative phases of his or her mixed methods study. The final step in choosing a mixed methods design is to locate the team members who will be able to help implement the mixed methods study. Some people may argue that this is not an essential step in choosing a mixed methods design, but we disagree. The members of one's mixed methods research team are essential to the design, because without the most appropriate and qualified people available and ready to assist, the mixed methods study may not happen (at all), or it may be a complete train wreck! To protect themselves and their resources, researchers should consider assembling an appropriate mixed methods team as a vital step in choosing a mixed methods design.

SUMMARY

In this chapter we have discussed some principles for designing a mixed methods study, decisions that should be considered when choosing a mixed methods research design, some of the more popular mixed methods research designs, and the details around each of those designs. Mixed methods scholars frequently suggest that there are "basic" mixed methods designs and more "advanced" designs, which extend the frameworks and philosophical underpinnings of the basic designs. We suggest that social workers interested in mixed methods research familiarize themselves with all of the mixed methods designs, their strengths and weaknesses, and understand these characteristics in the context of the social justice problem under study and the research questions. Due to the philosophical framing of the transformative design, we find that social workers tend to gravitate toward this design over the others, as it maintains the social justice lens that is germane to social work's mission.

3

"Third Floor": Mixed Methods Data Collection

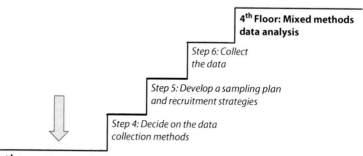

4th Floor: Mixed methods data analysis

Step 6: Collect the data

Step 5: Develop a sampling plan and recruitment strategies

Step 4: Decide on the data collection methods

3rd Floor: Mixed methods data collection

This chapter covers Steps 4, 5, and 6 of our nine-step process for conducting mixed methods research in social work. We begin with a discussion of the nuts and bolts of mixed methods data collection and how to choose the most appropriate methods for a mixed methods study. Next we provide brief descriptions of both qualitative and quantitative data collection methods, sampling plans, and recruitment strategies. Finally we present some commonly used data collection methods to ascertain qualitative and quantitative data. This chapter also differentiates between the types of qualitative and quantitative data that can be collected for a mixed methods study, as well as the conditions under which certain methods are appropriate.

DATA COLLECTION METHODS

Data collection methods are a set of procedures that are intentional and planned for the purpose of collecting a certain type and number of data sources that will be used to address a research question. A data source is the "who" or "what" that supplies the data. *Primary* (or firsthand) data are data collected from individuals or other sources who have experienced the topic of study more directly, while *secondary* (or secondhand) data refer to a more indirect account of a phenomenon. Specifically, this chapter covers selecting the data collection methods needed to answer specific research questions, determining the appropriate sample and recruitment strategies, and implementing appropriate data collection techniques to accomplish certain research goals.

STEP 4: DECIDE ON THE DATA COLLECTION METHODS

After choosing a mixed methods design, the next step in the mixed methods research process is deciding which data collection methods are needed. In actuality, one could argue that this step is more like Step 3(a) rather than Step 4—and we agree. The data collection methods that are used in a mixed methods study are frequently decided during the planning and design phases than during the data collection phase. In fact, by the time social work researchers reach the data collection phase, they have already made decisions about which data collection methods they want to use. Nevertheless, here we offer some strategies to help with choosing the most appropriate data collection methods to use for your mixed methods studies.

KEY ASPECTS OF THE STUDY THAT INFLUENCE THE METHODS

Social work researchers must anticipate (early on) the type of data they will need to answer their research questions and then choose data collection methods that will help them address these questions. Such planning at the front end of the study will save time and resources during the later stages. Considering certain aspects of research through a methods "lens" helps researchers decide on the most appropriate data collection methods. However, before we describe some common quantitative and qualitative methods used in social work, we first present key aspects of a study that may influence the decisions about which methods should be used to address the research questions. Among the most important are the size of the sample, the scope of the study, the support and participation of units or agencies, staff cooperation, resources, time, and previous research methods (For more on this, see Grinnell & Unrau, 2014). Each of these is discussed below.

Sample Size

When deciding on which data collection methods to use, researchers should consider the size of the sample because this can determine how long it will take to complete the project. The number of people, places, or cases represented will influence many different aspects of the project, including the data collection methods selected. Also, there may be different sample sizes that correspond to the quantitative and qualitative phases of the mixed methods study. For instance, a qualitative phase may consist of one-on-one interviews with 10 people (on a sensitive topic such as HIV contracted through rape), then the quantitative phase may involve 100 people completing a survey on the ways in which HIV can be contracted. Thus, the sample size for the methods selected can be a direct reflection of the research questions(s) addressed. If framed in an exploratory way, a qualitative phase would be necessary, while an explanatory question would likely require a larger quantitative sample.

Scope of Study

Data collection methods are also influenced by the scope of the research study. The scope of a research study refers to the breadth and depth of the problem being investigated. So social workers will need to ask themselves: Do different dimensions of the problem require different data collection methods? If so, that will affect the types of data collection methods they use for their research studies. The scope of a mixed methods study will help researchers decipher between whether a one-hour in-depth interview should be used to understand a particular topic or if a 90-minute focus group would suffice. Likewise, the scope of a study will also determine how open-ended or close-ended a questionnaire might need to be to capture the breadth and depth needed to answer a research question.

Support from Unit or Agency

The support, or "buy-in," of a unit or agency is important when it comes to the type of methods selected for a research study. For example, research studies that take place in agency settings should have the support of the agency director, manager, and program personnel on staff (Grinnell & Unrau, 2014). In some social work agencies, the practice (or "clinical") activities are apart from the social work research conducted within the unit. If the research and practice activities occur apart from one another, it is important to also consider how much overlap occurs between the clinical activities and the research activities. For example, researchers should avoid data collection methods that conflict with clinical philosophies or practices at the agency. The National Association of Social Workers' (2014) code of ethics also discourages this. Moreover, an agency's clinical records, archives, or other sources of existing (i.e., secondary) data may be especially useful and could help avoid duplicating data collection efforts. Yet this idea is null and void if the researcher does not have the support of the agency in which the research will occur. The bottom line is this: research methods are much easier to implement, and data are much more accessible, if supervisors and agency personnel are "on board" with a researcher's intentions and research plans.

Support from Staff

In addition to ensuring support by the unit or agency, researchers should make every effort to work cooperatively with the program staff, which includes being sensitive to their workloads. The primary goals of the staff at most human services units or agencies are not to support research. Instead, the roles and responsibilities of human service professionals are to provide services to clients, perform administrative duties, and/or complete other aspects of the job that keep the agency functioning. Social workers engaged in research at the agency level should think about ways to incentivize staff for their participation and be open to feedback from staff on the various stages of the research process. This is also a great way to build team morale. One way to incentivize staff is to offer job perks (e.g., meals, time off, financial bonuses) for their assistance with research projects. Further, feedback from staff about their experience during the research process can be collected using debriefing or summary reports so that the thoughts and feelings of the staff can be communicated to the research team at various stages of the research process. Similarly, whenever people at various levels of an agency participate in research, it is just good practice to share the research results with them.

Resources

Data collection can be expensive. The cost of survey instruments, materials, and supplies may influence which qualitative and quantitative data collection methods are chosen. Also, training people to collect the data is an additional expense as it requires space, food, time, and materials. Two other frequently overlooked expenses during the data collection process are transportation costs associated with data collection and data transcription. Transportation costs may require budgeting for fuel, mileage, and parking fees for team members who are collecting the data. Transcriptions rates can vary. Some professional transcriptionists charge by the hour, while others charge by line of text or by the word. Sometimes a highly motivated student can transcribe audiorecorded interviews, with a little guidance from an experienced researcher. Remember that the novice tends to *underestimate* the time it takes to collect data, the time it takes to transcribe it, and the costs involved with both. Therefore, social workers who are implementing a mixed methods research project for the first time would be wise to include a more experienced colleague on their team as a way to prepare for and address these challenges.

The mixed methods design for a research project can influence how the data for a mixed methods study will be collected in more ways than one. For example, budgeting for certain data collection–related costs will need to occur as early as possible, so that researchers do not need to worry about planning for these costs after the study has already begun. Costs can easily add up when budgeting for things like staff members' time (e.g., lead researcher, data collectors, data entry personnel, and office support), preparation for studying the research problem (e.g., training staff, reviewing the literature, analyzing existing data, and the primary data collection activities), and actual data collection procedures (e.g., implementing the sampling frame and recruitment). Costs are also incurred when deciding on aspects of the quantitative data collection methods such as reviewing potential survey measures, incentives, data preparation, equipment and supplies, data analysis, research dissemination, and overhead (e.g., costs associated with research facilities). See Table 3.1 for a breakdown of these cost-incurring items.

Time

Research projects often have designated end dates, or dates by which all activities associated with the research project must cease. These

Table 3.1. Sample Cost-Incurring Items

Measurement	• Scales and surveys owned by private agencies or other units may require a small fee
Data collection	• Hiring (at an hourly rate) project staff to collect the data, as well as the costs incurred with travel, meals, materials, etc.
Incentives	• Participant incentives such as gift cards, cash, meals, travel stipends, and child care
Data preparation	• Hiring transcriptionists and data entry staff
Equipment and supplies	• Recording equipment, name tags, pens, paper, binders, locked file cabinets, encrypted data storage
Data analysis	• Qualitative and quantitative data analysis programs and computer software packages
Research dissemination	• Printed materials for disseminating the findings; web hosting fees, web design fees, e-mail marketing, graphic design programs, design software
Overhead costs	• Building lease, electricity, water, central air/heat

deadlines are established by the immediate supervisors, the funding agencies, or perhaps the dissertation or theses chair and/or committee. Thus both internal and external time restrictions can influence one's choice of data collection methods. Researchers may also determine their time parameters, especially if they are using a brief version of a method or foresee challenges with extending a timeline for a project so that it overlaps with other projects.

Previous Research Methods

One of the most influential aspects for deciding which data collection methods to use is knowing what data collection methods were used by other researchers who have studied the problem (or similar problems) in the past. Therefore it is good practice to conduct a thorough literature review and learn from the existing research. By reviewing the methods from previous studies, one can get a sense for which qualitative data collection methods worked best to address the problem currently being investigated. Then the researcher can decide if the same data collection methods should be used again or if other methods should be used. To illustrate this, consider the use of a survey to collect quantitative data. If previous studies that have explored the topic of interest provided only binary response choices to the survey questions (i.e., "yes/no"), then developing a survey with more response options may be wise. By expanding responses beyond the binary and being inclusive of more ordinal (ranked) and/or interval (numerical) level data, researchers have the freedom to run more sophisticated analysis (Grinnell & Unrau, 2014; Melnyk & Morrison-Beedy, 2012; Russell, 2014).

QUANTITATIVE DATA COLLECTION METHODS IN SOCIAL WORK

Goals for quantitative data collection are to minimize error and maximize the response rate. The types of quantitative data collected for a study will usually depend on the research question(s) posed, the type of instrument(s) used, the researchers' relationship with respondents, the adequacy of data coding, and the accuracy of data input (Grinnell & Unrau, 2014; Rubin & Babbie, 2010; Russell, 2014). In social work research, as well as social science research more broadly, surveys are popular quantitative data collection methods. Here we present four common survey delivery approaches: mail, telephone, in-person, and Internet.

Mail Surveys

Mail surveys are best used when the data will be collected cross-sectionally (or at one point in time). Also, when trying to collect quantitative data from large samples, mail surveys are highly useful, as they offer the option of mass mailings (pending time and resources) with the hope that they will be completed and returned in a timely manner. Mail surveys are relatively inexpensive and are useful when no probing or follow-up detail is needed. Mail surveys are favored as a data collection method for social work researchers in particular because no interviewer bias is introduced and they allow for anonymous responses from study participants.

Despite the benefits of a mail survey, there are several challenges. For example, the overall increase of "junk mail" has made mail surveys a more difficult data collection method for researchers. Sometimes survey recipient may mistake a mail survey for junk mail and accidentally (or intentionally!) throw the survey in the trash. Another potential challenge with mail surveys is that despite their wide reach (i.e., mass mailings), the response rates are relatively low, suggesting that perhaps only highly motivated responders will complete the survey and mail it back.

Similarly, a certain segment of the population may not respond to a mail survey; surveys tend to be completed by individuals who read (i.e., literacy) at a certain level. Simply put, if potential respondents have trouble reading the survey, they are less likely to complete it, much less mail it back. One way to improve the response rates of mail surveys is to use closed-ended questions that are simple and require no explanation. Formatting and wording are also important, and the questionnaire should be short to moderate in length. Generally speaking, surveys that are no more than five pages long tend to fair better with potential respondents. Also, providing incentives for participants who return the survey is a useful tactic (Grinnell & Unrau, 2014; Russell, 2014), as this may also increase the number of *completed* surveys that are returned. Another way to increase potential response rates is to include a nice, clean cover letter on professional-looking letterhead.

After a pre-determined amount of time has passed, researchers can also use follow-up mailings to remind potential respondents to complete the survey, although more than two usually will not improve response rates.

The return rate for mail surveys is below 62% (Lin & Van Ryzin, 2012), so if researchers send out a mail survey and receive 65% to 75% back (and they are completed), they should consider that wonderful research karma! When calculating the response rate, researchers should not limit their response rate calculations to the percentage of surveys that were returned (e.g., 160 responses divided by 250 mailed is 64%). Instead, the number of surveys that would have not been completed in the first place should be included in the calculations (e.g., those who have moved, have died, or could not be found). Consider this example: if 250 surveys are mailed but 40 people are likely not to respond at all, then really only 210 surveys successfully reached their intended recipients via mail. In this case, the response rate is 76.2% (160 divided by 210), which is good.

Telephone Surveys

Another common survey delivery approach is the telephone survey. Since more than 90% of adults now have a cell phone (Rainie, 2013; for people under the age of 44, that number is closer to 97%), it makes sense. Telephone surveys are often conducted using random digit dialing, which allows for the collection of a large, representative sample. But there are other benefits to telephone surveys that make it an attractive option for social work researchers. For example, the use of telephone surveys can help the research team avoid travel costs and they can be easily monitored by supervisors, especially if each call is recorded. Telephone surveys also allow for follow-up (i.e., a callback if needed) and depth (oftentimes people feel more comfortable disclosing details from a distance than they do face to face). Telephone surveys may also be appropriate for youth and those with literacy challenges or low reading levels (Grinnell & Unrau, 2014; Rubin & Babbie, 2010). Telephone surveys, much like face-to-face interviews, allow for prompts, clarification, probing, and skip patterns.

Some disadvantages of the telephone survey are that the researchers collecting the data cannot see the facial expressions or mannerisms of the respondents, so they will likely miss nonverbal cues. Also, telephone surveys must be done in a shorter time frame; each should end after about 20 minutes (regardless of whether all of the questions have been answered). The success of a telephone survey usually depends on the verbal skills of both the respondent and interviewer. In addition, telephone surveys can sometimes be costly in terms of people's time and telephone charges (e.g., if certain telephone carriers do not offer free daytime, nighttime, or long-distance minutes). Some scholars argue that telemarketers have ruined response rates for telephone surveys and therefore encourage researchers to move away from telephone surveys to more Internet-based means of data collection. Another consideration is that in this era of smartphones, many people no longer have "land lines" (or they have caller ID) and will not answer calls from people they do not know. Technology-savvy people may prefer to text message potential callers rather than speak with them by phone.

In-Person Surveys

In a perfect world, every researcher would have the time, resources, and skill to administer in-person (or face-to-face) surveys to collect their quantitative data. In-person surveys have a high response rate (75%–90%) and allow for visual cues, which help illuminate communication between the interviewer and the respondent. In-person surveys require in-depth probing and follow-up if the responses provided by the participants are shallow or short. These surveys can last up to one hour and are very good for exploratory research. Despite the allure of an in-person survey, however, there are a few disadvantages. For example, while effective, in-person surveys can incur high costs and time for both the interviewers and the respondents. Another challenge may be the personal safety concerns of the interviewers (e.g., if they are working in particularly dangerous parts of the community that may have high crime rates). Along these lines, the interviewer's appearance may or may not affect (bias) the results of an in-person survey; likewise, social desirability as a result of an interviewer's gender, perceived age, attire, height, weight, and so on may be a concern. Therefore we advise researchers to consider the communities in which they plan to work (and seek advice from colleagues who have worked in these communities) before venturing into these communities to collect in-person survey data.

Internet Surveys

The growing popularity of electronic mail (i.e., "e-mail") or Internet-based surveys among some sub-groups is making quantitative data collection a more streamlined (and exciting) process for social work researchers. E-mail and other Internet-based surveys are fast and (fairly) easy to use to collect and organize data, as many programs now have systems in place that automatically import the data from surveys into a spreadsheet, making them instantly ready for cleaning and analysis. Internet-based surveys are inexpensive and can have a worldwide audience, if needed. With little to no inconvenience, social work researchers can create an Internet-based survey and send it out to hundreds (even thousands!) of people, in hopes that many of them will complete it. In some of our previous studies, we have used Internet-based survey programs that enter responses into a database and send an e-mail notification to the research team the moment a respondent clicks "submit." For these reasons, we are ardent fans of Internet-based surveys and have used them quite a bit in our own work.

Despite our enthusiasm for Internet-based surveys, we have also experienced their drawbacks. For example, while Internet-based surveys can be very useful, we have found that only computer-literate respondents complete them. So if a topic (and community) of interest includes individuals who may not be Internet-savvy, a researcher's ability to use the Internet for data collection (and maximize its benefits) with these individuals is limited. Also, from an ethical perspective, researchers who disseminate Internet-based surveys do not know who will *actually* complete the survey. For example, if a researcher's study eligibility criteria includes Asian women between the ages of 18 and 30, we can hope that only members of that group will complete the survey. However, if someone not fitting those criteria completes the survey, we would ever know. There are also no visual or verbal cues with Internet surveys, so if an explanation is necessary for any of the questions or response options, Internet surveys may not be the best survey approach. Three of our favorite (and cost-efficient) Internet-based survey programs are Qualtrics (http://www.qualtrics.com/), Survey Monkey (http://www.surveymonkey.com/), and JotForm (http://jotform.com).

Using Social Media to Collect Data

In this day and age, a plethora of technological tools can be used to collect data for research purposes. Related technological advances have been alluded to already in this section, but here we highlight the use of social media platforms for data collection. We have had experience using Facebook and Twitter as a means for data collection, particularly for our intervention projects. For example, one of our interventions involved using a Facebook group to deliver an education and social support intervention to young Black men. Given the popularity of social media for various forms of communication, it seems appropriate for researchers to think of the various ways to capitalize on Facebook's use in the daily lives of research participants. For example, we have found that young men from some communities are less likely to use a mental health professional when they experience mental health challenges. However, they are likely to get on Facebook and communicate their stressful life events and accompanying frustrations with their Facebook "friends." Thus we have found delivering mental health education and social support via Facebook is a useful way to reach young Black men whose mental health problems are less severe, who are less likely to disclose their challenges in public, and who are interested in acquiring more information about their mental health and masculinity.

In today's world of iCloud and Internet-based teamwork, web-based file hosting platforms and storage apps like Dropbox, Box, and Evernote can be especially accommodating for storing individual and team-based notes during the data analysis phase of a project. Similarly, we have noticed that several of our colleagues are beginning to use Twitter, Instagram, Snapchat, and Pinterest as ways to connect with their research participants and not only engage them in interventions, but also use these opportunities to collect data. Naturally, the types of data collected through various social media avenues can vary, and the beauty of such mediums is that these data can be extracted from the social media forums and imported into a database for analysis. We urge social work researchers to consider the possibilities that social media can offer in data collection and ongoing programming to benefit their clients and communities.

QUALITATIVE DATA COLLECTION METHODS IN SOCIAL WORK

Much like quantitative methods, qualitative research methods should be used when the research question calls for them. Recall that a qualitative research question might focus on participants' perceptions, impressions, or experiences regarding the phenomenon under study (Padgett, 2008). Here we discuss four of the more widely used qualitative data collection methods: individual interviews, focus groups, participant observation, and the review of existing records.

Individual Interview Methods

Individual interviews are at the heart of many qualitative research projects, where the research questions justify their use. The content of individual interviews often revolve around how people experience being a part of a culture or subculture, how they describe or comprehend an experience or event, or the discovery of regularities and patterns in people's experiences. Interviewers need to be trained on the components necessary for a thorough research interview. Interviews for research purposes are different from other types of clinical interviews or support group facilitation that is germane to social work, and there is guidance for how to proceed (Crabtree & Miller, 1999; Grinnell & Unrau, 2014; Russell, 2014). Despite being formally trained to conduct individual interviews, researchers should also be self-directed in their training and seek out various experiences to observe and participate in research interviews.

When developing the individual interview guide (or protocol), there are a few style options. The most popular interview styles are the unstructured (or "open") interview, the semistructured interview, and the structured interview. Unstructured (or "open") interviews tend to be free flowing by nature. They include few probes to guide the respondents' answers, and the probes are often generated by responses (e.g., they may or may not be written down prior to the interview). Semistructured interviews tend to be guided by a list of topics and subtopics that the interviewer uses to facilitate the interview. This allows the interviewer to modify the sequencing and wording of the questions to fit each particular interview situation. Standardized, more structured interviews usually consist of predetermined questions that are worded exactly how they are to be asked during the interview and leave little room for divergence from the interview guide (Grinnell & Unrau, 2014; Ulin et al., 2005).

Individual interview participants are usually not asked to select from a list of predetermined responses (like those in a survey), although there may be a research question that might benefit from some required responses as a part of the process. For instance, photo elicitation is an interview technique whereby respondents are shown photos and typically provide some information about what the photo evokes. Although this is usually a more free-form response, a respondent might be choosing a label or title for the photo—perhaps from a list. Specific probes are usually included in most interview formats and may be asked if needed at some point during the interview. However, in some styles of narrative interviewing the researcher stays out of the interview as much as possible, using only nods or encouraging gestures once the initial question has been asked. This style of interviewing is used when there is a specific way that the data are to be analyzed. The rationale for staying out of the interview is that respondents will usually find their own way to respond to a question, given the time and space. Note that silence, just as in clinical interviews, can serve a useful purpose in the qualitative interview, giving respondents time to gather their thoughts.

Finally, an unstructured, informal interview may occur spontaneously with a respondent during a field observation. This is the case in many ethnographic studies where the researcher is meeting individuals as they engage with the community under study. Audiotaping these interviews is not typical, and so the interviewer must be prepared to write up the interactions as thoroughly as possible later that day. With this method, fewer verbatim quotes are available. If there are multiple interviewers for a study, they must become comfortable working together as a team so that the intent of the research interviews and subsequent data analysis is established. Frequent meetings and feedback will help the team balance their own interviewer styles with the goals of the research to achieve uniformity (Crabtree & Miller, 1999; Padgett, 2008; Russell, 2014).

Focus Groups

By definition, a focus group is a group interview method that involves a skilled moderator who interviews 8 to 10 people in an environment that is conducive to sharing information (Grinnell & Unrau, 2014; Krueger & Casey, 2009; Morgan & Krueger, 1998; Padgett, 2008; Watkins, 2012). Interview questions asked during a focus group are usually predetermined; however, the moderator has a great deal of flexibility in asking follow-up questions and providing clarification and prompts. Many times, focus group questionnaires are open ended; they follow a logical sequence, from general to specific; and they tend to be exploratory in nature. The goal is often to gauge some general information or reactions to particular topics. Focus groups are conducive for collecting data about respondents' feelings and attitudes, experiences, knowledge, and beliefs.

Social workers use focus groups quite frequently and find them useful because they allow the researcher to capture a lot of data in one setting. The use of focus groups in a mixed methods study is a part of the mixed methods design, as it might be the first exploratory research activity conducted to get a feel for the types of responses that might a topic area might elicit. Focus groups might also help the researcher explore language idioms or create taxonomies for the construction of an individual interview guide. A focus group (or groups) may be used with different stakeholders at the end of data collection but before the final write-up to ensure that the developing themes have resonance with stakeholders (Krueger & Casey, 2009; Morgan & Krueger, 1998). Focus groups can also be used at regular intervals throughout a longitudinal project to keep the research questions front and center and to prevent drift from the original intent of the research. It is an opportunity to pause, refine, discuss, and interpret findings that may evolve over time.

A clear advantage of focus groups is that they represent a naturalistic data collection method, where participants tend to use one another to generate ideas and help develop the concepts that come out of the focus group interaction. Focus groups promote an atmosphere in which self-disclosure may feel safer, since the respondents are with others who resemble them in various ways. Researchers and respondents can view the data as they unfold, and there is real-time opportunity to ask questions or make corrections. Given the public nature of the discussions, focus groups may or may not be appropriate for research that covers sensitive topics; if the topic is sensitive, respondents are less likely to be as open and willing to answer questions. One example of this is a project that involved men and women discussing medication side-effects—the men's group was the only one to discuss sexual side-effects (a topic not specifically on the interview guide; Krueger & Casey, 2009; Morgan & Krueger, 1998).

In a mixed methods design, the focus group can be an important part of the data collection process. It may also yield research participants for individual interviews who are already familiar with the topic. Despite popular belief, focus groups are not necessarily a way to save time and money in a study, as they often require the same amount of both to produce data that will be useful for answering the research questions. They are also fraught with the same scheduling, recording, transcribing, and analyzing challenges of other qualitative methods. Different ethical considerations of focus groups must be considered as well. Note that the focus group must be mentioned in the final write-up of the project, as it helps other researchers understand what occurred in the study, in context; this reporting also represents part of the data audit trail (Crabtree & Miller, 1999; Russell, 2014).

Participant Observation

Participant observation usually happens in one of two ways: pure observation or engaged observation. With *pure observation*, the researcher remains separated from the group, event, or person being observed. This is more appropriate for use with nonverbal populations, as well as for studying different behaviors across different contexts. This kind of observation is a highly structured process that limits the number of defined behaviors that can be observed within a particular person, event, or phenomena (DeWalt & DeWalt, 2011). The other way in which observation can occur is when the participant is actively engaged with a group, called *engaged observation*. This is when the observer becomes actively involved in the research setting. This style of participant observation can make use of interviews that may vary across participants, given the topic under study (DeWalt & DeWalt, 2011; Grinnell & Unrau, 2014).

Review of Existing Records

As social workers, we often have access to data that has already been collected (also called existing records, archival data, or "secondary" data[1]) either in our work settings or through publicly available data sources (e.g., the Census Bureau). Paper and electronic documents, databases, patient records, case files, and other documented artifacts are all included in existing records. These records are valuable sources of information in social work research as they offer preexisting answers to many unanswered questions. Using existing records can save time, money, and other resources that could be lost should a researcher decide to initiate a new project that intends to collect data to which he or she already has access. The past few years has seen an uptick in the use of existing records that apply Photovoice and Photo Elicit in social work research (Moxley, Bishop, & Miller-Cribbs, 2015). Other helpful references for the review of existing records include Floersch (2000), who discusses the difference between what social workers write in charts and how they work with clients face to face, and Epstein (2010; in this pocket guide series) who outlines the advantages of clinical data mining.

STEP 5:   DEVELOP A SAMPLING PLAN AND RECRUITMENT STRATEGIES

Once researchers select the type of data collection methods needed for their project, they must develop a sampling plan to collect the data for the mixed methods study and finalize the recruitment strategy so they can collect data from the appropriate type (and number) of study participants. In this section we discuss how to develop a mixed methods sampling plan and recruitment strategies.

MIXED METHODS SAMPLING PLAN

Sampling for a mixed methods study is unique in that the researcher has two types of sampling strategies to consider. Likewise, depending on the design of the mixed methods study, these sampling strategies may or may not be directly connected to one another. Research aims for quantitative studies seek to develop a broad understanding of some aspect of the human experience. Subjectivity is not a goal in quantitative research. Sample sizes for quantitative studies are generally large because generalizability is the goal. By generalizability, we simply mean the ability to take a sample and apply the outcomes of the sample to the larger population. The sampling strategies for quantitative studies can involve various sampling techniques (e.g., simple random sampling), which are described at length by our colleagues (Grinnell & Unrau, 2014; Russell, 2014).

Compared to quantitative samples, sample sizes for qualitative studies tend to be small, as saturation (i.e., no new information emerges through data collection efforts) is the goal rather than generalizability. With qualitative studies, we continue to collect and analyze data until we see concepts that emerged previously in our study re-emerge. Sample strategies for qualitative studies are intentional; that is, the sample strategy should maximize the depth of a particular topic (not the breadth of a topic, as is the case for quantitative studies). Qualitative research tends to employ purposive sampling strategies. The goal with this type of sampling strategy is to acquire a sample that can yield rich knowledge about the topic under study. Social workers who use qualitative methods intentionally select the characteristics that they want included in their sample. They may choose elements of people, places, or things that they believe to be good sources of information, possess varied experiences, or represent extreme or deviant cases.

Popular sampling strategies in qualitative research are snowball sampling, deviant case sampling, and quota sampling (Grinnell & Unrau, 2014; Rubin & Babbie, 2010). With *snowball sampling,* the researchers ask the initial participants for help with identifying other participants who fit the participant inclusion criteria. This is very useful for locating difficult-to-access populations, such as people who are homeless, substance abusers, and members of stigmatized groups. *Deviant case sampling* tends to focus on cases that do not fit the usual pattern and may represent the extremes of the phenomena of interest. Sampling in this manner is useful because it involves identifying individuals who represent the purest or the most clear-cut instance of a phenomenon under study. For example, if we are interested in studying management styles in a grassroots organization, it would benefit us to study management styles within an organization that did exceptionally well and then study an organization that did not do exceptionally well to gain a sense of the outliers within this topic of interest. Finally, *quota sampling* applies to populations that have distinct categories of membership or participation. With quota sampling, the aim is to ensure that all subgroups of the larger population are studied. The quotas are likely designated by a research team, which has probably been given a quota to fill from specified subgroups of the community it serves. For example, an interviewer may be told to interview high-income Brazilian women between the ages of 45 and 60. Obviously quota sampling is not random in this case. Rather, the steps to draw a quota sample would be to (a) identify the key variables of interest and establish discrete categories of Brazilian women to sample, (b) determine the representation of each category in the population based on prior knowledge, (c) establish the desired sample size, (d) calculate the quotas, and (e) sample the population using convenience sampling or snowball sampling until the quotas are filled.

MIXED METHODS RECRUITMENT STRATEGIES

A mixed methods sampling plan is unnecessary if researchers do not have a clear sense of how they plan to recruit study participants. For example, it is not likely, in snowball sampling, that researchers know exactly how they will recruit each participant, nor will they have an exact number of total participants to write into the proposal. A useful strategy to consider when developing a recruitment strategy is to solicit help from gatekeepers who can provide an "insider's perspective" of the community in which the researcher plans to work. Gatekeepers in social work are important (Elpers & FitzGerald, 2013; Reamer, 1999, 2013), as such, gatekeepers in mixed methods research are also important, because they assist social workers with gaining entry to the communities and/or populations of interest (as well as gaining trust within these groups). Gatekeepers act as the bridges between communities and the researchers. Gatekeepers must be convinced that the research will produce more benefit than harm to their communities, that the participants' rights will not be violated, that the research will be sensitive to participants' needs and preferences, and that the researcher has adequate skills and resources needed to carry out the research as described (Elpers & FitzGerald, 2013; Reamer, 1999, 2013). Other recruitment strategies that can be particularly helpful for mixed methods studies in social work are recruiting through word-of-mouth and hanging flyers at social service agencies and human service units, providing colorful and eye-catching brochures and study placards, e-mail notices, and mass mailings.

For more information on developing qualitative and quantitative sampling plans and recruitment strategies that can applied individually, as well as collectively, in a mixed methods study, our colleagues have expounded on this for research specific to social work (Grinnell & Unrau, 2014) and in mixed methods studies more broadly (Creswell & Plano Clark, 2011; Curry & Nunez-Smith, 2015).

STEP 6: COLLECT THE DATA

After researchers have developed their sampling plan and recruitment strategies, the next step in the process is to collect the data. Ideally data collection will be performed by members of the project team. Specifically, we presume that the data collection for a mixed methods study will occur with a team of collaborators who have designated roles and responsibilities on the project. For instance, when conducting a mixed methods study, the lead researcher will likely have team members who are proficient with either qualitative procedures, quantitative procedures, or both (or the lead researcher may be skilled with both and require staff and trained assistants to *assist* with the implementation of the project). Regardless of who is designated to collect the data for the mixed methods study, researchers and team members must know the procedures for collecting data for both of the single-method phases (qualitative and quantitative) of the study. For this reason, it is imperative that someone with research experience (e.g., experience with the planning, implementation, and reporting of a project) be involved in the mixed methods study. This more experienced individual can provide a realistic framing of the plan and the way the team should proceed with data collection.

DATA COLLECTION FOR MIXED METHODS PROJECTS

In this pocket guide, it is not our intent to guide readers through the step-by-step processes for collecting the data associated with the individual qualitative and quantitative data phases of a mixed methods study. Other texts have outlined these processes in comprehensive ways (and specifically for social work), so duplicating the work of our colleagues here seems unnecessary. Instead, we opt to provide references that outline how to collect both qualitative (Darlington & Scott, 2002;

Padgett, 2008) and quantitative data (Grinnell & Unrau, 2014; Rubin & Babbie, 2010; Russell, 2014) separately and urge readers to look to these sources for information on how to collect data for the single-method phases of their mixed methods studies. This focus on each of the single methods helps ensure the rigor of the mixed methods study, for the quality of the data collected individually will have a major impact on the quality of the data for the mixed methods purposes. Therefore, and in lieu of outlining the processes involved in collecting separate qualitative and quantitative data, we offer some suggestions for researchers to consider as they plan for data collection in mixed methods studies. These considerations include conducting a pilot study, centering the data collection plan on the study design, developing a data collection protocol, and planning for participant retention.

Pilot Study

If time and money permit, we always recommend that researchers do a "test run" of the data collection method and other mixed methods study procedures by conducting a pilot, or "mock" study. This is an opportunity to carry out all aspects of the data collection plan on a smaller scale, before the large scale mixed methods study begins. The pilot test allows researchers to work out the "kinks" in the data collection plan in terms of process and outcomes, so that time and resources will not be wasted once they are ready to implement the large scale plan (Melnyk, Morrison-Beedy, & Moore, 2012). Data collection methods can also be tested in less formal ways. For example, researchers can try out a particular aspect of data collection with their study team, or even with individuals not involved with planning the study, for example by running a few aspects of the study by them (e.g., the wording of the interview questions) and/or by gauging people's reactions to the words used in a questionnaire. Asking multiple people to view the study procedures and data collection plan prior to implementation is a good idea.

After the pilot test, researchers can then use the feedback from the pilot to improve the data collection procedures. A process evaluation of the pilot can help to determine whether the researcher was thorough in his or her efforts, starting from obtaining participant consent and ending with the actual data collection procedures. Doing this pilot test of the study from start to finish can give researchers a sense for the process.

Did it seem as though you had everything you needed during data collection? Did it feel like you were maximizing your time with participants? A smooth data collection process requires this kind of proactive planning. Also, pilot data are critical if seeking additional funding, as oftentimes funding agencies want to know if a study has been attempted on a smaller scale before they invest money into it.

Study Design

When it comes to collecting data for a mixed methods study, researchers may also consider collecting data based on the study design. To do this, they will need to determine the timing of the qualitative and quantitative data collection phases based on the ordering of the methods in the mixed methods design. For example, if a researcher is using an exploratory sequential design, then he or she will collect qualitative data first, followed by quantitative data. In this example, researchers will need to proceed with the sampling plan and recruitment strategies for the qualitative phase of the mixed methods study with the understanding that they or their team will also need to allow enough time (and resources) to recruit and collect data for the quantitative (i.e., second) phase of the study. In addition to timing, and under certain conditions, some quantitative and qualitative data collection methods may be selected over others. For example, if the research budget is limited (in terms of time and money), social workers may opt for a less time-intensive or less expensive data collection method (e.g., an online survey as opposed to a face-to-face survey).

The novice social work researcher may develop a very rigid project timeline that consists of steadfast dates by which he or she plans to recruit, screen, and consent participants for a study. However, the more experienced social work researcher will develop a project timeline and factor in some "cushion" time in case things do not work out as intended and/or there are challenges with certain aspects of the recruitment, screening, and consenting procedures. We frequently tell social work students and colleagues to tack three to four months onto their final project timeline, as this is usually enough leeway to account for potential challenges (and surprises!) that may arise during the data collection phase of a study.

Data Collection Protocol

For many social work settings, documenting the methods used for research are important for duplication and evaluation. Thus it is often necessary to develop a mixed methods study manual, with a protocol for how the procedures will occur. When developing a research protocol, it is especially important to include details for how the data will be collected; such an outline can include the measures that will be used to collect the data, when the data will be collected, how the people responsible for collecting the data will be trained, what data will be collected, any equipment needed, as well as any frequently asked questions that could assist future team members with research-related activities (Melnyk & Morrison-Beedy, 2012). Given the nature of the research, the study protocol could also include guidelines for issuing payments for study personnel and participant incentives, as well as safety protocols (i.e., emergency numbers and contacts) (Grinnell & Unrau, 2014). We have also found it useful to include details for how our research methods (and scales) are standardized and administered, as well as details for how the project "chain of command" should occur (i.e., how the project should be supervised). Ethical considerations can also be added to study protocols, as well as recommendations for how to establish an audit trail (how a third party can review the evidence), and the importance of journaling (i.e., keeping a notebook of rules and decisions that were made, reasoning, and thinking), and other aspects of the project.

Although they may not be included in the study protocol, here, we provide some other factors that should be considered when working with teams to collect data for mixed methods research in social work settings. These include the needs and expectations of the project staff (i.e., work habits and preferences); suggestions for record keeping and document/data sharing (i.e., what, when, and by whom); and suggestions for ways to enter, manage, and store the data (as well as how, by whom, and when). As suggested, it is good practice to document every single detail of a study. We deem this important to note because most researchers see the value in documenting the larger, more obvious aspects of their projects (e.g., the data collection plan and recruitment sites), but few consider also documenting the more minor aspects (e.g., the number of staff members needed to implement one aspect of the project, the recommended competencies of interviewers, etc.). In addition, proposed project timelines can also be useful, as a framework for the most ideal times of the year (and the amount of time required) for data collection and analysis. This level of detail will be especially useful to colleagues who may oversee the project in later years.

Hiring and/or Training Data Collectors

Over the years we have learned that good data collectors (e.g., interviewers) are sometimes few and far between. Therefore we offer some considerations for hiring and training the team members who will be responsible for collecting the data for projects. First, when hiring people to collect data, several characteristics should be considered. For example, the education and language skills should be top priority. Given that the primary purpose of data collectors is to collect data from people, researchers will want to ensure that they identify data collectors who have the education and level of language skills appropriate to do this. Also, depending on the geographic location of the research sites, requirements such as a valid driver's license, access to and use of a car, and proof of insurance, as well as references and a background check, may be essential for data collectors (Grinnell & Unrau, 2014).

Researchers will also want to ensure that the data collectors they hire have some experience with the population of interest; that they understand participant confidentiality; and that they agree to abide by research's code of ethics and standards. Sometimes, given time and resources, researchers may have to hire data collectors who have no prior knowledge or experience with the population and/or no familiarity with the code of ethics. In these cases, researchers should conduct an extensive training for the data collectors so that they are knowledgeable and prepared before they begin their work. Be explicit in what data collectors are trained on; topics can include an orientation to the unit or agency in which the research will occur; an overview of the study; reflexivity (or, the interviewer's position in the research); self-awareness during interviews, including voice, posture, facial expressions, body language, and attire; and principles of empathy for and rapport building with research participants. Pending time and resources, researchers may even want to offer opportunities for the data collectors to learn and practice their interview skills during training, as well as their time management by providing opportunities to engage in such skills before they interact with participants.

Plans for Retention

Retention is defined as the ability to retain individuals over time. Attrition, on the other hand, is the loss of study participants over time. Attrition is very common in all types of research, because people move, lose interest, or sometimes die before the study is completed. This is just the nature of research with human subjects. Despite this, however, some strategies can be used to retain research participants. For example, social work researchers can develop rapport with participants. This often overlooked (yet highly effective) strategy could mean the difference between having a sample size of 10 versus a sample size of 50. Research participants are people too; therefore, they want to feel as if their participation is needed and wanted, and, more important, that their absences are noticeable. Another strategy for reducing attrition rates and increasing retention rates is to develop a good tracking system or database. Simply asking for the contact information for important people in the lives of your research participants, such as partners, relatives, and friends can make tracking them down during a later phase of the study much easier. Also collecting different types of contact information, such as e-mail addresses, and work telephone numbers can minimize the likelihood of attrition. Generally speaking, minimizing the potential burden of the research participants can increase their likelihood of participating throughout the duration of the study. Estimating the time for participation and sticking to the estimates as much as possible, as well as providing reimbursements for time, can help retain research participants. For example, offering incentives and child care during the study testing period may seem minor, but it can go a long way in the eyes of the research participants.

SUMMARY

This chapter began by outlining how the research question can influence the decision to use qualitative methods, quantitative methods, or both in a research study; the decision regarding *which* methods to use; and the decision regarding the characteristics of the study sample. There are both strengths and limitations to quantitative and qualitative data collection methods, but it is the complementary nature of these strengths and limitations that make mixed methods research such a rewarding experience for social workers interested in addressing some of the world's most complex social justice concerns. A large part of the mixed methods research process for social workers is not only knowing how to conduct research but having a plan at the forefront of the mixed methods study. This should include the most appropriate quantitative and qualitative data collection methods to use, a plan for testing the entire data collection process (using a pilot test), a plan for how participants will be sampled, and a plan for how to address potential challenges as they arise.

NOTE

1. *"Secondary data"* is also the term used to describe data that researchers have not collected themselves, but to which they have access, and are using for research or evaluation purposes. Usually, someone else (e.g., a colleague or a different research team) has collected these data; thus, it has become a "secondary" data source. Although the researcher may not have been initially responsible for this secondary data source, there may be aspects of it that are valuable to a mixed methods study. Given the nature of this text, we do not expound on this very much. However, we have experience with using secondary qualitative and quantitative data sources and have received internal and external funding for mixed methods projects that utilize secondary data sources.

4

"Fourth Floor": Mixed Methods Data Analysis

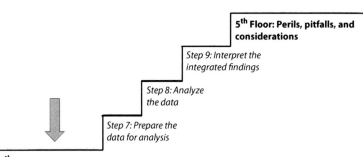

5th Floor: Perils, pitfalls, and considerations

Step 9: Interpret the integrated findings

Step 8: Analyze the data

Step 7: Prepare the data for analysis

4th Floor: Mixed methods data analysis

This chapter covers the final three steps of our nine-step process for conducting mixed methods research in social work. We begin by describing how to prepare qualitative and quantitative data for analysis. Next we provide some helpful techniques for efficiently coding and analyzing qualitative data, then we transition into a basic description for how to analyze quantitative data and how it can be used to obtain descriptive statistics (such as crosstabs, frequencies, and distributions), measures of central tendency, measures of variability, and measures of association. We also briefly discuss how to maximize rigor and the relevance of analysis procedures for analyzing qualitative and quantitative data. We end this chapter with some useful tips on the actual "mixing" of mixed methods research, the various points in time during which mixing can occur, and the ways data can be integrated and interpreted.

STEP 7: PREPARE THE DATA FOR ANALYSIS

PREPARING THE QUALITATIVE DATA FOR ANALYSIS

Step 7 of our mixed methods process involves preparing both the qualitative and quantitative data for analysis. Preparing the qualitative data for analysis in a mixed method study is not unlike preparing the data for a single-method, qualitative study. Researchers should begin by making a list of all the data they want to include in their analysis, then arranging all of the data they plan to include in the analysis in a format most conducive for the analysis. For example, various types of qualitative data can be represented in a format called a transcript. A transcript is a written record of the interview, discussion, focus group, or meeting that was held to understand the phenomenon of interest. In short, it is the written (or typed) record for any experience that has been documented for research purposes. It consists of more than merely the words spoken by each interviewee. It may also include notes to reflect nonverbal communication such as pauses, laughing, or crying. Developing a transcript for the qualitative data is important if one is preparing to conduct a qualitative data analysis. Researchers must decide if they want to transcribe the data themselves or have someone else do it.

Regardless of who transcribes the data, certain factors are important. For example, qualitative data are quite extensive. It has been estimated that just one 60-minute interview can generate as much as twenty pages of text! So it is essential that research teams decide who should transcribe the data. Should the researchers do it? an intern or student? a professional transcription company? If the researcher or someone from the team decides to do it, they should plan for a ratio of approximately 1:3;

in other words, for every one hour of recording (i.e., an interview, a focus group, a meeting), plan for about three hours for the transcription. When writing a proposal to fund a mixed methods study, researchers must budget for the cost of transcription and accompanying equipment (e.g., transcription foot pedal, headset, speakers, transcription software), especially if the researcher or a team member will be responsible for transcribing the data.

Format the Qualitative Data for Analysis

After the qualitative data are in transcript form, the transcripts need to be reviewed to ensure that there are no errors. Not until after this occurs can researchers begin formatting them for the analysis. The researcher or a member of the research team can do this. Whoever is chosen for this task should be detail-oriented and have a keen eye for catching errors. Whenever we format transcripts for analysis, we always find it helpful to use the automatic line numbering feature of our word processing software and to create wide margins for notes and comments. Figure 4.1 is a snapshot of a sample transcript from one of our projects. When formatting the transcripts for analysis, one should not forget to consider the ethical issues that may arise from handling personal data (we discuss this further in chapter 5). For example researchers should consider using aliases or participant numbers (in lieu of real names) to protect the identity of research participants. Also, identifying information should not be included in the transcript (e.g., birth dates, telephone numbers, email addresses, mailing addresses), as this would violate the confidentiality promised to research participants during the consent process. Finally, the identity of individuals must be concealed when using quotes or describing text data in the final report.

Finalize a Qualitative Data Analysis Technique

While still preparing the data in transcript form, we also find it useful to finalize the anticipated data analysis technique. Oftentimes this decision is easier to finalize after we see the kind of data that we have and what aspects of the data need to be analyzed to address specific research question(s). In other words, we always have a strong inkling for the type of qualitative data analyses techniques we want to use during the study

	IRWG	LOW	June 22, 2010

57 **PARTICIPANT 29**

58 Nothing good ever happens with me, nothing good is ever gonna happen.

59 **MODERATOR**

60 That's what they say, that's what depressed men say?

61 **PARTICIPANT 29**

62 I mean I think.

63 **PARTICIPANT 30**

64 I'm never gonna get this job. They're not gonna hire me cause I got a felony.

65 **WHAT CAUSES DEPRESSION**

66 **MODERATOR**

67 *So that's a great transition into my next question which is what causes*

68 depression?

69

70 **PARTICIPANT 32**

71 Loss of hope and just giving up, giving up and low self value, not realizing what you are.

72 **PARTICIPANT 29**

73 Vary of circumstances (low audio, didn't pick up)...

74 **PARTICIPANT 31**

75 Loss of self esteem. Feeling hopelessness. Lack of not caring. Distrust. A real deep loss.

76 When you lose something real bad you just go into a deep depression.

77 **PARTICIPANT 33**

78 Negative energy. People who come and actual will tell you that you cant do something and it'll

79 make you start believing it and uh yeah.

80 **PARTICIPANT 27**

81 I was about to say something just like that and it's a combination of just like you feeling like you

82 are not worth it and then people reinforcing that by telling you you're not worth it.

Figure 4.1. Sample transcript.

planning phase, but this idea is usually solidified after we have collected the data and begin formatting it for analysis.

Constant comparative analysis, content analysis, and narrative analysis are a few examples of common methods used to analyze qualitative data (Leech & Onwuegbuzie, 2011; Miles, Huberman, & Saldaña, 2013). Although constant comparative analysis is a staple element of the grounded theory approach, it is probably the most common form of qualitative data analysis more broadly. It involves developing a system to reduce the transcribed text data to codes and then linking and unlinking those codes to create larger themes. In essence, constant comparative analysis is a means to sort and sift the data to manageable units that have meaning (and often full definitions, if creating a code book) that make sense to the research team (Miles & Huberman, 1994; Miles et al., 2013; Padgett, 2008).

Content analysis utilizes some quantitative data transformation from a simple counting of codes to a formula for determining code density (Miles et al., 2013). Many researchers convert their qualitative data into frequencies and percentages to tell the story of research participants. This is often called "quantifying" qualitative data. Though this is a popular qualitative data analysis technique (particularly among more experienced quantitative researchers who are trying their hand at qualitative projects), we usually approach such data conversions with caution or try to avoid them altogether. Narrative analysis involves analyzing the data with particular attention to participants' stories. The story itself is the unit of analysis and is often given the same critical read as if one were reading a book or a play. Narrative analysis can be evaluative when one is telling one's own story, and it can be linguistically analyzed with the researcher's question in mind, as the respondents give meaning to their lives.

Decide Between Traditional or Computer-Based Analysis Methods

While finalizing the qualitative data analysis technique, researchers should also decide if they want to use computer-assisted qualitative data analysis software (QDAS). For example, some researchers may decide that they want to conduct their analysis using the traditional "cut-and-paste" method, which involves paper, scissors, and tape, although nowadays, with the help of computers, this method is rarely used. Instead, researchers opt for using an electronic cut-and-paste strategy with word processing programs (i.e., Microsoft Word). Regardless, researchers who have access to QDAS tend to use it for managing, organizing, and coding their data. Atlas.ti, Ethnograph,

Dedoose, and NVivo are popular QDAS packages used by agencies and organizations. However, to save money and reduce the amount of time needed to learn new software packages, qualitative researchers have also opted for programs in the Microsoft Office Suite such as Microsoft Word and Excel to organize, manage, and analyze qualitative data for analysis (La Pelle, 2004; Niglas, 2007; Stockdale, 2002; Swallow, Newton, & Lottum, 2003). Regardless of the QDAS package used, a researcher should never forget that he or she is the actual "tool" in qualitative data analysis (Watkins, 2012). We expound on what we mean by this next.

Researchers as the "Tools" in Qualitative Data Analysis

While some scholars would argue that statistical software packages are necessary tools used to generate quantitative results, QDAS packages are also tools, though they are used in a slightly different manner than statistical software packages. With QDAS packages, we, as the researchers, are the "tools" used to generate the qualitative results. In other words, there is an intuitive step when generating both quantitative and qualitative results; however, this step is more expanded and iterative when dealing with qualitative data. As mentioned, due to the expense associated with QDAS packages, some qualitative researchers have turned to tables and spreadsheets created in Microsoft Word and/or Excel (La Pelle, 2004; Niglas, 2007; Stockdale, 2002; Swallow et al., 2003) for their qualitative projects. Those who advocate the use of Microsoft Word and Excel suggest that these programs provide the features needed to assist the user with moving from transcript pages to codes and themes for reports efficiently and affordably (Watkins, 2012). Moreover, it is not necessarily the programs themselves but rather how users apply the features of each program that make them effective for the organization, reduction, and analysis of qualitative data (La Pelle, 2004; Niglas, 2007; Stockdale, 2002; Swallow et al., 2003; Watkins, 2012).

Using computer-generated tables and spreadsheets to organize and reduce qualitative data is not new to data analysts. In fact, as long as electronic tables and spreadsheets have been around, students and researchers have employed them to organize, manage, and present their qualitative data (La Pelle, 2004). Although electronic tables and spreadsheets are used to organize and reduce qualitative data, novice qualitative researchers may assume that, like quantitative software, the user can just "input" qualitative data into the QDAS package, enter a command, and *voila!* The program will automatically generate the results. This is false, and in fact, due to the nature of qualitative inquiry, this is not even the intent of the qualitative data analysis process. Earlier we alluded to the quantification of qualitative data and cautioned readers about this technique. While it can be used to achieve some qualitative research goals because it exhaustively explores the data, ensuring that frequent trends (e.g., emphases, repetitions) in the data are included in the analysis, the quantification of qualitative data should be approached with caution and should not be overemphasized. In other words, qualitative data should not be treated as if it were quantitative (Sandelowski, 2001). The misuse of frequency data in qualitative analysis is problematic and is not the sole intent behind the use of electronic databases to assist with qualitative data analysis. Instead, QDAS packages were meant to act as coproducers of the qualitative results. One could even suggest that QDAS packages are "costars" of the analysis process because the researcher is the true "star" of the show.

Data tables and spreadsheets can serve as tools in the data analysis process, working in conjunction with the intuitive examinations and interpretations of the data analysts. It is the responsibility of the qualitative researchers to "analyze" the data—the software will not (and cannot) do it for them. This may be a deterrent for the novice qualitative researcher, as the analysis of qualitative data is sometimes not as clear and straightforward as that of quantitative data, which can provide more direction through the use of formulas and predetermined algorithms. Analyzing qualitative data is an intuitive process that takes time and several attempts, as the analyst must become familiar with what the data presents, acknowledge the relevant themes, and organize the themes based on the research questions (La Pelle, 2004; Watkins 2012). I (DCW) am an advocate for using Microsoft Word and Excel to leverage these steps. The advantages of using electronic tables and spreadsheets to organize, reduce, and analyze qualitative data have been acknowledged elsewhere (La Pelle, 2004; Niglas, 2007; Stockdale, 2002; Swallow, et al., 2003). Likewise, the capabilities of the software have been highlighted, including the ability to review rows and columns of otherwise cumbersome data and identify, compare, and highlight relevant codes, concepts, and themes (Swallow et al., 2003).

With the increase of qualitative research in social work there is a growing need for more convenient and efficient ways for organizing, reducing, and analyzing qualitative data. Therefore, for many of my (DCW) qualitative and mixed methods projects, I use Microsoft Word or Excel as my database and an analysis technique that I have developed and polished over the past 10 years called the "rigorous and accelerated data reduction" (RADaR) technique for qualitative data analysis. The purpose of the RADaR technique is to generate data tables that produce qualitative results quickly and rigorously for translation and dissemination to intended audiences. The RADaR technique is implemented using a team-based analysis approach (Fernald & Duclos, 2005; Guest & MacQueen, 2008; Watkins, 2012), and it was developed for the purpose of analyzing various types (e.g., focus groups, interviews, case studies, existing documents, etc.) and quantities (e.g., 5 case studies, 12 individual interviews, 8 focus groups, etc.) of qualitative data to efficiently generate results that can be incorporated into one or two specific project deliverables. These project deliverables can range from peer-reviewed manuscripts for scientific journals to a thesis, dissertation, final project report, conference presentation, book chapter, and/or health promotion materials.

Before beginning the RADaR technique, analysts should have already completed some of the preliminary, preparatory steps for team-based qualitative data analyses that have been described elsewhere (Fernald & Duclos, 2005; Guest & MacQueen, 2008; Padgett, 2008; Watkins, 2012). The nature of the RADaR technique implies that it should be used as a tool for—and in conjunction with—completing other steps of team-based qualitative analysis. For example, the RADaR technique can occur after the team revisits the research question and becomes "one" with the data (Taylor-Powell & Renner, 2003; Watkins, 2012) but before the team develops the data's "open codes" (Grinnell & Unrau, 2014; Ulin et al., 2005; Watkins, 2012). Tables and spreadsheets developed in word processing, and accompanying general purpose computer programs (Niglas, 2007; Stockdale, 2002; Swallow et al., 2003), are the basis for the RADaR technique, as they tend to encourage the user to focus more on the content of the data and less on the bells and whistles that QDAS packages may offer.

PREPARING THE QUANTITATIVE DATA FOR ANALYSIS

Now that we have covered some steps to consider when preparing qualitative data for analysis, we will now cover a few steps associated with preparing quantitative data for analysis. Researchers and their teams must ensure that before the quantitative data are analyzed, they must be arranged in a quantitative database, cleaned, and coded. We describe each of these tasks next.

Develop a Quantitative Database

If a researcher has finished collecting surveys and has a pile of them sitting on his or her desk, what should he or she do? Well, the next step is to develop an electronic database to help the researcher manage, organize, and (eventually) analyze the survey data. A quantitative database is a grid that specifies all of the variables. This database also allows researchers to set up columns so that each question or item can have its own column heading. After that, every subsequent column can be a response to a question from the survey and every row can represent a case or respondent from the survey. These databases can be created using Microsoft Excel, the Statistical Package for the Social Sciences (SPSS), or another data management program.

Clean the Quantitative Data

After the database has been created, a logical next step is to "clean" the quantitative data. By "cleaning" the data, we mean double-checking the accuracy of the data and then arranging the data in the database in a way that is clear and concise. Essentially, double-checking the data means checking it for errors. While researchers perhaps cannot fathom the idea that their data will have any errors, mistakes are very common within quantitative databases. Errors can occur from entering the data incorrectly into the database (e.g., accidental "slips of the finger" occur all the time), or the errors may be specific to the way the study participants answered the questions on the survey. Other human error, such as data being entered on the wrong line, can also occur. Data cleaning also involves looking to see if some data are wrong given the possible response options. For example, consider the question: How satisfied are you? If responses are on a 5-point scale and one of the responses entered into the database is an 8, then chances are that the 8 was entered in error. For larger quantitative data sets, frequency tables can be used to identify possible outliers. For smaller datasets, we often just "eyeball" the database to identify any potential errors or data outliers that were entered in error.

Code the Quantitative Data

After developing a quantitative database, entering the quantitative data into the database, cleaning the data and checking it for errors, researchers must decide if they should recode data for the purposes of the analysis (and to answer the research questions). Researchers may decide to collapse some survey items or create additional categories within the database. This is often done when some attributes have only a few responses or when it makes theoretical sense to collapse some items so that there are fewer options to analyze and compare. For example, if numbers of certain racial/ethnic groups are low, they are often collapsed into a category called "other."

The next step in preparing the data for analysis is developing a way to process the data. This is where quantitative "codes" become important. Researchers must code the data in a way that tags each portion with a meaning that links the database to the items in the survey. For example, names and labels can help identify and organize the data. In quantitative databases, value codes are also created. For example, if a sample includes both men and women, men may be coded as "0" and women as "1." These are also called *dummy codes*. Age is another variable that is often used in quantitative studies and is often calculated in actual years. Scores on a depression scale can be coded as an individual response to an item (e.g., 1 to 5) or as the total depression score (e.g., actual sum of all items is 1 to 20). How satisfied clients may be with social work resources can be coded using their actual scores on a satisfaction survey (e.g., 1, 2, 3, 4, 5, 6, and 7).

When cells (or, the individual boxes in a database where the columns and the rows come together) are empty, this can easily seen novice researchers into a panic. There are a number of different ways to handle missing data, one of which is to code the empty cells as 99 or 999. These numbers are frequently used to take the place of actual scores because they are unique and help indicate this is a true missing value and not a data entry error. For more information on how to handle missing data, see other social work research texts that cover this in detail (Grinnell & Unrau, 2014; Li et al., 2014; Rosenthal, 2012; Rubin & Babbie, 2013; Weinbach & Grinnell, 2009).

Using software packages like SPSS allows researchers to create a *data view* or a *variable view* in which they can add more details to the quantitative database and variable descriptions. This level of detail can come from the actual survey text and can help the researcher (and future team members) understand question construction, response options, and other details about the survey. After the data are coded, the researcher or someone from the team should go through the database and conduct another round of "cleaning," just to ensure that that there are no errors derived from the participants' input or any human errors, such as entering the data on the wrong row or line. Again, a slip of the finger is very common, so "eyeballing" the data is always a good idea.

STEP 8: ANALYZE THE DATA

Arguably, the most important step of any research study is the data analysis step, which is the eighth step in our mixed methods research process. As a rule of thumb, researchers should ensure they have a plan for how they will analyze the qualitative and quantitative data for the mixed methods study sooner rather than later. Keep in mind, however, that the quality of a mixed methods study is not determined by simply the *inclusion* of both qualitative and quantitative data; rather, it is determined by the *rigor* with which a researcher completes each phase of the study—especially the data analysis phase. In Step 8, we describe how to analyze the qualitative and quantitative data in a mixed methods study, beginning with the qualitative data analysis.

ANALYZING QUALITATIVE DATA

The purpose of qualitative data analysis is to sift, sort, and categorize the data in such a way that the researcher ends up with themes that will ultimately help answer the research question(s). Qualitative data analysis usually involves the analysis of words, or "text data." For example, researchers who plan to include a qualitative component in their study are anticipating the analysis of written documents, spoken and recorded words from interviews, and observational notes. Just about anything that can be documented and labeled (using text) can undergo a qualitative data analysis. Although there are dozens of references that describe ways to analyze qualitative data (e.g., Auerbach & Silverstein, 2003; Bernard & Ryan, 2009; Krysik & Finn, 2013; Miles et al., 2013; Padgett, 2008; Rubin & Babbie, 2013; Saldana, 2012; Silverman, 2011; Ulin et al., 2005), there is no one "right way" to analyze qualitative data. Given the space limitations of this pocket guide, we only provide an overview for how a social work researcher conducting a mixed methods study may want to analyze the qualitative data for his or her study. However, for more in-depth guidelines and set of procedures for analyzing qualitative data, see the previously mentioned sources and those in our Reference list.

Simply put, qualitative analysis is the process of labeling, organizing, and extracting meaning from text data. In particular, qualitative analysis labels what was *said*, what was *observed*, and the *researcher's thoughts and reflections* about these words and observations. Despite the plethora of steps for analyzing qualitative data, we find the qualitative analysis procedures recommended by Grinnell and Unrau (2014) and Watkins (2012) concise, cohesive, and of great use. Below, we provide our adapted version of some of the most important steps. First, researchers must *establish an initial framework and plan of action* for how they will analyze the qualitative data. It is wise to decide on this plan before the data analysis begins so the research team can have a strategy in mind.[1] The second step is to *develop "open" codes and then more "focused" codes*. This is the part of data analysis whereby researchers begin to attach meaning to the text they are analyzing. Finally, researchers must *look for meaning and relationships among the codes*. We describe these steps in more detail and the subsequent tasks involved next.

Establish an Initial Framework and Plan for Analysis

When analyzing qualitative data, the first task is to establish an initial framework and plan for the data analysis. The initial framework may likely be guided by the qualitative research questions or an in vivo style of analysis. When an initial framework is guided by research questions, researchers outline the types of concepts (and codes) they will use to analyze and organize the data. When using in vivo style of analysis, they allow the concepts and codes to emerge from the words of the study participants. We frequently use both styles for the initial framework, as we want to establish a framework that is both derived from our research questions but also allows for flexibility where we can include concepts that are best derived from our participants' words.

A second part of establishing a framework and plan for analysis is deciding on an analysis plan. What has worked particularly well for us over the years is to first preview the data and then document our ideas about the data with a diary or journal. Researchers must become familiar with all the data prior to analyzing any parts of it. We affectionately call this "becoming one with the data" (Watkins, 2012). During this process, researchers should resist the temptation to interpret the data, as the true purpose for the preview stage is to learn the "flow" of the data, to explore the nature of the verbal exchanges (if applicable), and to gauge any data patterns. As reviewing pages and pages of qualitative data can be cumbersome, we frequently use various points of entry when reading qualitative data. For example, if there are three 20-page focus group transcripts, we suggest researchers not begin on page 1 for each transcript every time they review the data but rather begin on page 1 the first time they review all three transcripts, then during the second pass begin on page 5, then during the third pass begin on page 10, and so on. Of course using this strategy to become one with the data will take some time, so researchers need to allow plenty of time for reviewing the data.

Next, it is a good idea to use a diary or a journal to record analytical memos (i.e., overall thoughts about certain aspects of the data). When doing this, researchers should always record the date of the memo, as it can be interesting to see how they and other team members feel about different aspects of the data throughout the data analysis process. Researchers should also document any references, reactions, points of confusion, and other important sources in the diary, journal, or in a centralized team database. We always try to label our memos and others journal notes with descriptive headings and use diagrams in memos to explain our initial framework and plan for analysis. In these journals we avoid restricting the content of our notes and instead allow for a free flow of ideas and unfiltered reactions to the data.

Perform Open and Focused Coding

After establishing an initial framework for analysis, the next step involves coding the qualitative data. Coding involves marking portions of the qualitative data with labels to designate which portions of the text fit with the identified categories. Next to specified words or sentences, research teams can write brief comments that provide insight into the importance of those elements. Keep a running log of in-depth thoughts, concerns, questions, and ideas about certain concepts that stand out during the coding process. Coding qualitative data is a two-step process that contains various levels of complexity (Grinnell & Unrau, 2014; Watkins, 2012). The first step involves establishing "open" (or first-level) codes, and the second step involves refining the open codes into "focused" (or second-level) codes.

To develop *open codes*, researchers must first read through the data, identify chunks of text that convey similar meanings, group these chunks of text together, and then assign them to categories. Often these categories (or open codes) will frame the concepts used to label the analysis. When developing open codes, keep in mind the two types of coding that we alluded to earlier in this section: coding guided by the research questions and in vivo (or participant-driven) coding. Coding that is guided by research questions is sometimes referred to as *etic* (or outsider) coding, and in vivo coding is sometimes referred to as *emic* (or insider) coding. With etic coding the researcher has an underlying theory in mind regarding the themes presented in the data. Etic coding often occurs as a direct result of the qualitative research question or the concepts that one hopes to uncover in the qualitative analysis. With emic coding, the researcher does not assume any underlying theory ahead of time; categories emerge directly from the data. To ensure a successful open coding experience, we recommend that readers follow the steps suggested by Grinnell and Unrau: (a) identify chunks of text that convey similar meanings, (b) identify categories (or open codes), (c) assign chunks of text to categories, (d) refine and reorganize coding, and (e) decide when to stop.

Identifying chunks of text that convey similar meanings is the first task of the open coding process. During this task, researchers review transcripts for chunks of data (i.e., words, sentences, or paragraphs) that convey specific ideas or have particular meaning (Grinnell & Unrau,

2014; Watkins, 2012). Next they *identify categories,* which simply means grouping chunks of data together with a common thread, or open code. During this process, researchers may find that constant comparison analysis is particularly helpful as it allows them to compare and contrast meaning units to assess similarities and differences across the data (Leech & Onwuegbuzie, 2011). Constant comparison analysis allows one to code an initial set of text data then use the code applied to the initial set of text data to code the remaining text data. For instance, using an example from earlier in this chapter: if one is applying constant comparison analysis to three 20-page focus group transcripts, one may decide to create emic and etic codes from the first transcript, develop a codebook, and then use these codes (and the codebook) to code the remaining two transcripts.

Qualitative data categories can be simple or complex depending on the depth and breadth of the analysis. Therefore, after researchers have identified categories to which they will assign the chunks of data, they will then *assign the chunks of text to these categories* (Grinnell & Unrau, 2014; Watkins, 2012). During this task, codes may evolve into abbreviated category names. For example, an open code like "mother's past service use" may very well evolve into "MPSU." After assigning chunks of text to the categories, or open codes, researchers should *refine and reorganize the coding system* that they developed. Essentially, this final task in the open coding process is a chance for researchers to pause and reflect on the logic and strategy used to draw meaning from the data thus far in the analysis. This procedural pause can be used as an opportunity to change coding strategies, collect more data, or make other changes to the initial framework and data analysis plan. The final task in open coding is *deciding when to stop.* Deciding when to stop coding the data is always a thorny subject for researchers. However, most experts recommend stopping when data and category saturation has been achieved (Bernard & Ryan, 2009; Krysik & Finn, 2013; Miles et al., 2013; Padgett, 2008; Rubin & Babbie, 2013; Saldana, 2012; Silverman, 2011). This means researchers should stop coding when data categories (or codes) fit easily into the current analysis scheme and no new categories surface from the analysis.

After the open coding process is completed, the next step is to develop more *focused codes.* This level of coding is a more in-depth, second-level process of coding that is more abstract and gives meaning to the initial, open codes (Watkins, 2012). Focused coding involves two distinct tasks: (a) assigning (and reassigning) chunks of text into categories and (b) comparing categories. Assigning (and reassigning) chunks of text into categories refers to designating which pieces of transcripts or text data can be set aside for further analysis and inclusion in the final reports. In a traditional qualitative data analysis sense, this would involve the act of (literally) cutting and pasting pieces of the transcripts that researchers annotated by the open code categories into a secondary file designated as "focused" (and eventually "final") codes. This is a process of reorganizing the data by "lifting" and "separating" coded data from the transcript. In some of my (DCW) undergraduate anthropology classes, this process would involve spreading 8-inch-by-11-inch copies of interview transcripts on the tables in our anthropology laboratory, cutting out portions of text with scissors, and placing these sheets on the wall or other open space (the floor works too!) so that we could compare and contrast our various data concepts and connections. Index cards can also be used to achieve the same goal of grouping the data that meet certain code criteria and answering the research questions. However, today many researchers use computer programs and/or QDAS packages (e.g., Microsoft Word, Microsoft Excel, NVivo, Atlas.ti, Ethnograph, etc.) for this process.

Look for Meaning and Relationships Among the Concepts

The final step in qualitative data analysis is looking for meaning and relationships within the data. This involves comparing categories, which involves examining the focused codes from the analysis to see if patterns and themes exist among individuals or between groups of individuals in the study. For example, in looking for patterns and themes in the qualitative data, Grinnell and Unrau (2014) suggest that qualitative analysis teams consider temporal relationships (*A* precedes *B*), causal relationships (*B* is the consequence of *A*), and nested relationships (*B* is a part of *A*). We agree, and note that looking for meaning and relationships in qualitative analysis involves looking for the "story" in the data that can help answer the research question(s).

While coding and analyzing qualitative data, researchers should frequently question how they and their team members are seeing the emerging patterns or themes in the data and how these themes relate back to the original research question(s). Look for deviations from the themes in the data, areas of disagreement, and contrasting concepts. Search to identify the factors that can help explain the deviations (but keep in mind that this may mean returning to the field for additional data collection). Remember that saturation is the goal here—in other words, making sure every stone has been overturned (so to speak) when searching for the answers to the research question(s). A helpful strategy in moving from data coding to comparing categories is to organize the codes, themes, and data patterns that were uncovered from the analysis into data displays. These may come in the form of Venn diagrams, web diagrams, tables, or figures, or they may look very much like the mixed methods design diagrams we discussed in chapter 3. The major difference between the mixed methods design diagrams and a qualitative data display is that, in the latter, we are trying to visually represent the relationship between qualitative codes, themes, and subthemes (if applicable).

When looking for meaning and relationships during qualitative data analysis, researchers must also interpret the data and build theory from the findings. For example, developing visual representations from the data are important for moving certain areas of inquiry forward (Grinnell & Unrau, 2014; Miles et al., 2013; Ulin et al., 2005). In addition, when presenting themes or theory and moving the research forward, researchers may decide they want to rephrase their themes into questions, develop new hypotheses, and/or pose a new theory based on the findings from the qualitative analysis. (Remember the knowledge-level continuum we discussed in chapter 1.) This is a perfect illustration for how social work research can come "full circle." However, despite the temptation to keep stakeholders waiting in order to collect more data and/or perform additional analyses, the research *must* stop at some point. Stopping is necessary to move the research further. However, for the sake of the research team and the stakeholders, researchers should be sure to note when the data categories have been sufficiently defined and always document their own thinking processes to assist in moving the qualitative analysis from description to interpretation.

Maximize Rigor

Maximizing the rigor of an analysis involves judging whether the conclusions that have emerged from the analysis are credible, defensible, and able to withstand alternative explanations. Over the years we have found that the easiest way to have people disregard (or, worse, disrespect) our qualitative research, data, and findings is to not demonstrate the rigor of our qualitative research process. One of the reasons for the increase in the number of published qualitative studies is the growing interest and the widespread acknowledgement of the contributions that qualitative methods makes to research. Some journal editors have even allocated space in each issue of their journals for such exploratory and in-depth studies. Qualitative studies have a greater chance of being published if they are conducted rigorously and reported as such (Miles et al., 2013; Watkins, 2012). One way to demonstrate the rigor of qualitative research is to demonstrate and report how various aspects of the study are *credible, dependable, confirmable,* and *transferable* (Lincoln & Guba, 1985; Ulin et al., 2005; Watkins, 2012).

Validity in quantitative research is the extent to which the measurement diverges from (or toward) the concept it intends to measure. *Credibility* is the corresponding criterion for qualitative research (Ulin et al., 2005; Watkins, 2012). Credibility focuses on confidence in the truth of the findings, including a precise understanding of the context. The question that should be asked to ensure that the qualitative study is credible is: Do the findings show a logical relationship to one another? In other words, are the findings consistent with regard to the outcomes they support? Credible qualitative studies are those in which the findings are grounded in, and substantiated by, the data (Lincoln & Guba, 1985; Miles & Huberman, 1994; Miles et al., 2013; Ulin et al., 2005; Watkins, 2012); although this is not to say that if one's study does not achieve this, one cannot collect more data.

For qualitative researchers, reliability, or the extent to which study findings can be replicated, is impractical. In other words, it is highly unlikely that qualitative researchers can replicate the findings from their qualitative studies even if the research design is replicated perfectly. Instead, qualitative researchers should strive for the *dependability* of their qualitative findings, not the reliability. Dependability is whether the research process is consistently carried out with careful attention to the rules and conventions of qualitative methods and methodology (Ulin et al., 2005; Watkins, 2012). Questions that are aligned with a study's dependability include: Are the research questions clear and reasonably connected to the research purpose and design? Are there similarities and parallel features across data sources? Do multiple project team members have comparable data collection protocols? (Lincoln & Guba, 1985; Ulin et al., 2005).

Confirmability is the qualitative analogue for objectivity in quantitative research (Lincoln & Guba, 1985; Watkins, 2012). Confirmability implies that an adequate amount of distance exists between the observer and the observed and minimizes any possibility of the data inquiry being influenced by the observer. The qualitative researcher must know that even as a coparticipant in the inquiry, he or she has maintained the distinction between personal values and those of the study participants (Ulin et al., 2005). When the concept of reflexivity is applied, the researcher is obligated to document his or her own role in the research process, including assumptions, biases, or reactions that might influence the collection and interpretation of data (Lincoln & Guba, 1985; Ulin et al., 2005). Reflexivity can contribute to the confirmability of qualitative research results. *Transferability* in qualitative research is synonymous to generalizability in quantitative research. Ulin and colleagues (2005) suggest that lessons learned in qualitative studies can be applicable to other situations if samples have been selected based on their applicability to the viewpoints and experiences that are expressed in the research problem.

Researchers should always ensure that their qualitative data analyses are performed rigorously, for the sake of the stakeholders, the credibility of the research team, and the respect for the study findings. Several methods can be used to maximize rigor (Grinnell & Unrau, 2014; Lincoln & Guba, 1985), and in Table 4.1 we present five: triangulation, respondent validation, an explicit account of the data collection and analysis methods, reflexivity, and attention to negative cases. Grinnell and Unrau (2014) posit that another important aspect of ensuring the rigor of qualitative data analysis is assessing the trustworthiness of the results by establishing credibility, documenting what has been done to ensure consistency, and documenting what has been done to control biases and preconceptions (see also Lincoln & Guba, 1985; Ulin et al., 2005).

To establish credibility in the final report or write-up of the qualitative results, consider noting the research qualifications of the team, their training and experience, and the method of recording data analysis procedures. Documenting what has been done to ensure consistency is a large part of assuring the rigor of one's work. This involves providing a context for how data were collected, triangulating multiple perspectives

Table 4.1. Checklist to Maximize Rigor in Qualitative Data Analysis

☑ *Data triangulation*—Make an effort to compare results among different methods of data collection or different sources.

☑ *Respondent validation*—Review results of the data analysis with the participants of the research; apply "member checking" techniques.

☑ *Account of the data collection and analysis methods*—Provide an explicit description of how the data were collected and analyzed.

☑ *Reflexivity*—Reflect on the researcher's position in the research; mainly, how the researcher might have directly impacted the research process and conclusions.

☑ *Attention to negative cases*—Provide evidence that aspects of the data that seemed to contradict conclusions were explored, cases that differed from the norm were sought, and rival explanations for the findings were considered.

Adapted from Krysik and Finn (2013).

(e.g., data sources or researchers), and using member checking (e.g., going back to the data source) to ensure that the information, as reported, is accurate in their eyes. Over the years we have found that documenting every aspect of the analysis process has been essential to the success of our qualitative analyses and encourage readers to monitor this portion of the research process closely.

Documenting biases and preconceptions can be achieved by purposefully examining the data for meaning that is different from what one believes or from themes already detected, reflecting on one's own actions as an interviewer, and looking for negative "evidence" (Grinnell & Unrau, 2014; Watkins, 2012). Other comprehensive qualitative analysis techniques for social work research can be found in other texts from the Social Work Research Methods Pocket Guide Series (Epstein, 2010; Longhofer, Floersch, & Hoy, 2012; Oktay, 2012; Wells, 2011) and those outside of the series (Grinnell & Unrau, 2014; Padgett, 2008; Ulin et al., 2005). Next we discuss steps associated with the quantitative data analysis process.

ANALYZING QUANTITATIVE DATA

Now that we have covered the steps associated with analyzing qualitative data, we will now discuss steps for analyzing quantitative data. The purpose of statistics is to convey meaning about how certain variables (e.g., the independent and dependent) do or do not (or to what extent) relate to each other (Rosenthal, 2012; Weinbach & Grinnell, 2009). We begin our section on analyzing quantitative data with a discussion about how to analyze quantitative data to acquire basic, general descriptors of the information gathered, called *descriptive statistics*. Then, we cover the ways in which statistics are used to test hypotheses about similarities, differences, or relationships between and among variables, called *inferential statistics*. Although we do not endeavor to provide comprehensive guidelines for how to analyze statistical data and conduct statistical analysis in this pocket guide, we do provide an overview of some common computations that social workers who are conducting mixed methods studies may consider including in their quantitative study phases. But first, we begin with an overview of descriptive statistics.

Descriptive Statistics

The nature of descriptive statistics is that they are used to provide a basic, descriptive understanding of the data. Descriptive statistics are obtained by first understanding that the purpose of the data analysis is to help tell a story about the data. Researchers may decide to begin with trying to discover what is common among the data. For example, a researcher may find that all of the respondents to a survey are between the ages of 30 and 50 and that most of them have improved outcomes after some intervention. A question to pose at this point may be: What is the extent of difference or variation among this sample? For example, incomes for respondents from the data may be between $11,000 and $60,000, and respondents' attitudes about certain items on the questionnaire may vary based on their income.

With descriptive statistics, researchers have the potential to acquire information about measures of central tendency, variability, position, and the distributional shape of the data (Onwuegbuzie & Combs, 2010). Statistical analysis that are descriptive can also help frame the characteristics of one study variable at a time, thus providing a "snapshot" of the data. Essentially, descriptive statistics allow us to get a sense of the data while helping us decide if additional analyses are needed. For example, scatterplots are used to identify outliers when one is trying to acquire a quick understanding of the data. Scatterplots help identify data that are not consistent, or are out of alignment, with other aspects of the data. Researchers may then need to determine whether there is an error in the data entry or the recording of the data and how they should handle those errors. Before we discuss analyzing qualitative data any further, we pause here to briefly discuss levels of measurement, which are necessary for understanding how variables are operationalized and analyzed using statistical procedures.

Levels of measurement are determined by variable attributes, which are the characteristics or qualities that describe a variable. Variable attributes can be defined at four different levels of measurement: nominal, ordinal, interval, and ratio. The lowest level of measurement is *nominal* level-data; attributes or response categories of a nominal level of measurement variable are mutually exclusive, meaning that everyone who completes the survey must fall into one of the response options. For example, two different options for the question "Where do you live?" could be (a) in-state and (b) out-of-state, and respondents must select one of these options. *Ordinal*-level data are the second highest level of measurement. Attributes or response categories for an ordinal variable are mutually exclusive (just like nominal variables), but they are also rank ordered (Grinnell & Unrau, 2014). The example that we tend to use when we are teaching about ordinal variables is the standard grading system in schools: A, B, C, D, and F. This is a great example because when selecting from these responses, it is assumed that all respondents will choose one response (which meets the "mutually exclusive" requirement), and it is obvious that there is a ranked order between each of the responses (i.e., A is a higher grade than F).

Interval-level data are the third highest level of measurement and have response categories that are mutually exclusive, rank ordered, and an equal distance from each other. (Notice that each level of measurement builds on the features of the previous one, then it includes one new, additional feature.) An example of interval data can be the responses to a question such as "How happy are you with your child(ren)'s school principal?" with response options on a Likert-scale from 0 (meaning "not happy at all") to 5 (meaning "very happy"). Interval-level variables must be in an order whereby the same distance exists between each of the response options. In this example, one child determines the difference between each of the five options.

The final level of measurement is *ratio*-level data, which are considered the highest level of measurement because these data encompass all of the features of the previous levels of measurement, with one additional feature: these data are based on a "true" zero point. In other words, the attributes or response categories of a ratio variable are mutually exclusive, rank ordered, an equal distance from each other, and based on a true zero point. For example, for a question like "How many children do you have?" rather than providing options for the respondents, we could just leave a blank line or a space for the respondents to write in a number. Allowing "0" to be in option allows us to have a starting place for analyzing these data, but there are no upper limits on the number that a respondent can write in. Thus if someone were to write that he or she had 13 children, this would be an allowable response (for a very busy family!).

Measures of Central Tendency

The most common descriptive statistics are measures of central tendency. There are three types: mode, median, and mean. Table 4.2 lists these three statistics and the corresponding levels of measurement that are used to acquire each statistic. We do not describe details regarding how each of the measures of central tendency are computed here and instead refer readers to statistical texts that include information on how to compute these (e.g., Grinnell & Unrau, 2014; Rosenthal, 2012; Weinbach & Grinnell, 2014). However, for the purposes of understanding the range of options offered via descriptive statistics, we provide a basic overview for each below.

The *mode* is the most frequent value that appears in a set of values. The mode may be used to answer questions such as "How many times per year do clients visit the domestic violence shelter in the city?" The mode is often used by social work researchers seeking frequent values

Table 4.2. Level of Measurement, Statistic, and Corresponding Questions

Level of measurement	Statistic	Corresponding question
Nominal	Mode	What is the most frequent value?
Ordinal	Median	What is the middle score?
Interval/Ratio	Mean	What is the average?

Table 4.3. Sample Mean calculation for 10 participants

P1	P2	P3	P4	P5	P6	P7	P8	P9	P10
1	2	2	1	4	2	1	3	2	1

How to calculate the mean:
1 + 2 + 2 + 1 + 4 + 2 + 1 + 3 + 2 + 1 = 19
19 divided by 10 (number of participants) = 1.9
Mean = 1.9

Note: P = participant.

that emerge in their data, and there are different types of modes. For example, while unimodal data involves distribution with one mode, in bimodal data two values are most frequently reported. Along the same lines, multimodal data includes more than two values.

The *median* is the value that divides the distribution in half. For example, if one were to line up each score from a list of 21 intervention participants from highest to lowest, the eleventh score would be the median score. In other words, 50% of scores would be on each side of the eleventh score, which is the median score. If there are an even number of values (e.g., 18, 20, 22, etc.), the median would be the average of the two most central values after they were arranged from highest to lowest. Median computations are most useful if extreme scores impact the mean (e.g., income or age).

The *mean* is an average of all the scores. This is the most popular measure of central tendency, as it is the sum of the values divided by the number of values. For example if 10 intervention participants all scored 1's, 2's, 3's, and 4's in a distribution like the one provided in Table 4.3, the total sum of all the scores would be divided by the number of participants ($n = 10$), which would result in a mean of 1.9. Means are useful to ascertain because for some statistical analyses they can be substituted for any items that are missing (i.e., for questions that a respondent may have left blank).

Measures of Variability
Measures of variability help to ascertain how widely a value or values are distributed across a sample or a population. This is a measure of dispersion. There are two types of measures of dispersion: the range and the standard deviation. The *range* is the distance between the minimum

and maximum score in a distribution; the larger the range, the greater the amount of variation in scores in a distribution. The minimum level of data needed to calculate a range is ordinal data. An example of a question that can be asked to achieve a range of scores is: What are the highest and lowest values?

The *standard deviation* is a mathematically calculated value that specifies the degree to which scores in a distribution are scattered, or dispersed, about the mean. The standard deviation is an accurate and detailed estimate of dispersion because an outlier can greatly exaggerate the range. Standard deviation is used to compare the variability of distributions and to interpret scores in the normal distribution. The standard deviation demonstrates the relationship of the entire set of scores to the mean of the sample. The mean in standard deviation defines the basic properties for a normal curve, and the minimum level of measurement needed for a standard deviation or any standard deviation calculation is interval-level data.

In summary, descriptive statistics can help researchers organize the data for further analyses. The first level of analysis involves some basic organizing of the data, which may include tasks such as tallying and counting or running a crosstabs analysis in a statistical software program. Typically, the analysis results in cases being placed into groups. Researchers need this baseline information about the data to see if additional analyses that inquire about causal relationships and associations are necessary. These additional analyses are called inferential statistics.

Inferential Statistics

If descriptive statistics allow the researcher to organize or summarize data to give meaning or facilitate insight, then *inferential statistics* are methods that allow inferences to be made from a sample to a population (Weinbach & Grinnell, 2014). We begin our discussion with what makes inferential statistics "inferential."

Statistical Inference
Statistical inference is the process of estimating population parameters from sample statistics (Grinnell & Unrau, 2014; Rosenthal, 2012; Weinbach & Grinnell, 2014). Statistical inference occurs when a sample is first picked from the population. Then the research team collects data

from this sample with intentions to infer, or generalize, the findings from this sample to the larger population from which the sample was selected. In order to make accurate and reliable generalizations about the larger population, the sample must reflect the population and the characteristics under study. So, for example, if 30% of our sample prefers cotton candy over other food options at the local carnival, then it would be safe to conclude that 30% of our population also prefers cotton candy. Statistical inference may be used to ascertain whether differences exist between groups, and, as you know, these differences can be gender-based, race-based, income-based, education-based, ability-based, and so on.

Statistical inference tends to use a calculation called the p value to achieve most of its goals. The p value is the probability that a relationship between variables or a mean difference found in a sample is a result of sample error. In other words, we tend to use the p value statistic to determine whether the relationship exists, but what the p value really tells us is how much of that statistic is due to chance. For example, the commonly used p value cutoff of .05 means there is a 5% chance that the relationship between the variables is due to sample error. Another way of thinking about this is that there is a 95% chance that the relationship is *not* due to sample error, and the differences in the sample actually reflect the differences in the population. We tend to reject the null hypothesis if the p value is less than .05, and this means that we accept the alternative hypothesis (we expound on this terminology later in the chapter). Despite what statistical inference can tell us using the p value, sometimes the sample does not reflect the population. There are some influences on sample error, such as luck, sample size, and homogeneity. For example, someone can win the state lottery even if the odds are 40 million to 1 (here's hoping!). With regard to sample size, smaller samples tend to calculate more chances of error than larger samples. Finally, with homogeneity, we find that less variation within the population (and thereby within the sample) yields smaller sample error. (Again, we provide more information about this later in the chapter.)

Types of Inferential Statistics
Next we move into a discussion about the types of inferential statistics that can be used to infer information about the relationship between variables. In the following paragraphs, we provide a brief description

of parametric statistics and nonparametric statistics which helps determine how much (at under what assumptions) we can infer findings from our sample to the larger population.

Parametric statistics. Parametric statistics are used when we want to compare the means of two or more groups that are relative to the variance within those groups. Parametric statistics can help researchers estimate the value of the population parameter from the characteristics of the sample (Rosenthal, 2012; Rubin & Babbie, 2013; Weinbach & Grinnell, 2014). Although parametric statistics are commonly used by social science researchers, there are certain assumptions that must be met in order to use them correctly. For example, the use of parametric statistics assumes that the values of a sample are normally distributed and that at least one variable is at the interval or ratio level. In other words, surveys that use only nominal and/or ordinal levels of measurement may violate the assumptions of parametric statistics and should be approached with caution. For more information on the conditions under which parametric statistics are most appropriate to use, see Rosenthal (2012), Rubin and Babbie (2013), and Weinbach and Grinnell (2014).

Nonparametric statistics. If, given the characteristics of the data set, the plan for analysis cannot be completed because certain assumptions for parametric statistics would be violated, then researchers should consider using nonparametric statistical tests. With nonparametric statistics, we are usually comparing the medians or ranks of two or more groups. Also, nonparametric statistics are more forgiving of the underlying distributions of the sample and when the data meet the assumption for nonnormally distributed data, which is often found with nominal or ordinal data. Oftentimes the samples for nonparametric statistics are not random and are small (which is often the case with convenience samples or samples from social work interventions). Deciding whether to use parametric statistics instead of nonparametric statistics is often determined by the types of data available based on the levels of measurement. For example, a researcher may ask questions about one's chances of getting a flat tire on the way to work, whether a new movie will be ranked number one during its opening weekend, or (for a more social work–relevant issue) the chances of knowing that a child will be safe if he or she is left in a home where there has been a previous report of child abuse. One's use of nonparametric statistics to answer these questions may depend on the variable attributes or response categories used to answer the questions (i.e., levels of measurement).

Hypothesis Testing

Hypothesis testing is a statistical test of an expected relationship between two or more variables. With hypothesis testing we tend to first establish a "null" hypothesis (H_0), which means that there is no relationship between the variables under study. An example of this might be: There is no relationship between education and mental health. In addition to the null hypothesis, we also establish an "alternative" hypothesis (H_1). One type of alternative hypothesis is the two-tailed hypothesis, which is used to establish that there *is* a relationship between the variables under study. Using the same scenario, we could say that an alternative hypothesis would be: There is a relationship between education and mental health.

Another type of alternative hypothesis is called a one-tailed hypothesis, which means there is a directional relationship between the two variables under study. Using the above example, we could say: The greater someone's educational level, the better his or her mental health. In hypothesis testing, we test the relationships between two or more variables by using statistical tests that determine the probability that the relationship between variables is due to sampling error or to chance. In Table 4.4, we illustrate the types of hypotheses that we use to determine if relationships between variables occur due to sampling error or

Table 4.4. Hypothesis Types and Examples

Hypothesis type	Description	Example
Null hypothesis (H_0)	Suggests that there is no relationship between the variables of interest	There is no relationship between parental income and child delinquency.
Two-tailed hypothesis (H_1)	Suggests that there is a nondirectional relationship between the variables of interest	There is a relationship between parental income and child delinquency.
One-tailed hypothesis (H_1)	Suggests that there is a directional relationship between the variables of interest	The greater the parental income, the greater the child delinquency.

chance, mainly the null hypothesis (H_0); the alternative hypothesis (H_1), which may determine that that there is a relationship between the variables; and a directional hypothesis (H_1), which suggests the direction of that relationship. Which of these alternative hypotheses should be used will be determined by whether one selects a two-tailed or one-tailed test (see, e.g., Cornelius & Harrington, 2014; Dattalo, 2008; Orme & Combs-Orme, 2009; Randolph & Myers, 2013, for additional details about these types of tests).

Hypothesis testing involves the decision around whether we want to reject the null hypothesis (and accept an alternative hypothesis). The decision constitutes an inference that we make about a population based on our calculations from the sample of that population. If the p value is less than .05, we reject the null hypothesis and accept the alternative hypothesis. Commonly accepted levels of chance are $p < .01$ (1 in 100) and $p < .05$ (5 in 100). There are also two types of errors involved in this decision-making. With a Type I error we reject the null hypothesis but no relationship actually exists among the variables. This will happen 5% of the time if the rejection level is .05. This is when we say there is a relationship, but we are wrong. (See Table 4.5.) With a Type II error we do not reject the null hypothesis but the relationship actually exists among the variables. A Type II error is always possible because statistical "power" depends on sample size and type of statistical test. It is harder to find significance with small samples and nonparametric tests, although the rejection level can be adjusted if there is insufficient power. This could be due to sample error or low rejection level. We may say there is *not* a relationship, but we would be wrong. This is what we mean by the "power" of a statistical test; we want this probability to be large. (We provide more information about statistical power later.)

Table 4.5. Hypothesis Testing Decision Table

Decision \ Reality	Null hypothesis (H_0) is true	Alternative hypothesis (H_1) is true
Reject (H_0)	Type I error (α) usually .05 or .01	Correct decision (Power = $1 - \beta$) usually .80
Do not reject (H_0)	Correct decision ($1 - \alpha$) usually .95 or .99	Type II error (β) usually .20

For hypothesis testing, we want to first state the null hypothesis and then state the alternative hypothesis. Next we need to decide on the direction for the alternative hypothesis and whether it is one-tailed or two-tailed. (We provide examples for both one-tailed and two-tailed tests in Table 4.4.) At that point, we should then set the level of statistical significance associated with the null hypothesis (Type I error) and select the appropriate test statistic. We will then need to compute the test statistic value and determine the critical value needed for rejection of the null hypothesis for the statistic (if appropriate). We should then be prepared to compare the obtained value with the critical value. As a final step, we make a decision regarding whether we should accept or reject the null hypothesis.

Hypothesis testing is very common during the quantitative phase of a mixed methods study; however, there are some common pitfalls with hypothesis testing. First, because we tend to use language like "significance" to determine the likelihood that an effect is due to chance, it can be assumed that the significance of variables also translates to their importance. But let us be clear: statistical significance is not the same as importance. For example, moving from drinking 30 beers per day to 24 beers per day may evoke a statistically significant difference, but it is not a clinical improvement, in relation to one's health. Another common pitfall is misunderstanding the role of the p value. The p value does not signify the strength of the relationship, but rather it shows the chance of a Type I error. With a large sample size, even a small association may have a low p value (or a p value less than .05). So the p value does not confirm the hypothesis; it only indicates that sample error is unlikely. Thus hypothesis testing provides only a preliminary look at whether an error is likely, with the assumption that we will proceed with additional tests. With hypothesis testing, other sources of error are not ruled out.

Other pitfalls are "fishing" for statistical significance. Science suggests that at .05, one in every 20 tests will show statistical significance by chance. If we run hundreds of tests, we are likely to get several significant results by chance. Thus researchers should not "fish" for statistical significance but rather let the research question and research objectives guide the direction of the analyses. Another common pitfall is assuming that statistical significance infers causation. It does help us determine Type I and Type II errors, but it does not tell us which came first. Researchers must establish what came first, but they also need to rule out any extraneous variables. Significance testing (due to the aforementioned factors) tends to be misinterpreted as a test of importance and causation. Due to the role of sample size (n) in the formula for parametric statistics, a large sample size can make a negligible difference between groups appear significant.

Statistical Power

Next we take a brief, albeit necessary, tangent to provide more information about statistical power. *Statistical power* is the probability that a statistical test will detect a statistically significant effect. Though, an actual power analysis helps the researcher to obtain an adequate sample size for his or her pending study. It lets us know how many people should be included in the study so that the findings can be generalizable. We need to know how many people we need to include in our final analysis so that we can know exactly how much we can infer our statistical findings onto a larger population. Prior to conducting a study, researchers should conduct a statistical power analysis. If this is not a skill that they possess, then they should consult with a statistician or someone who is more proficient with this type of analysis.

Statistical power is important to consider because it helps the researcher and the audience interpret the statistical results. The power of a statistical test is represented as one minus beta ($1 - \beta$), and is influenced by some parameters, such as the significance level, the sample size, and the effect size. Each parameter has a direct and positive relationship with statistical power. For example, as significance levels (alpha) decreases numerically, power decreases as well. As effect size increases, power increases, and as the sample size increases, so does power. The larger the true magnitude of the effect in the population, the greater the power of a statistical test to detect it. The larger the sample size, the greater the power of the test. So beyond simply going out and collecting survey data, power gives us a sense for under what conditions we can actually infer what we find after administering a survey to a sample from a larger population.

While on the topic of surveys, we also want to briefly mention the importance of knowing whether a predetermined scale was used in a survey prior to the analysis. If a scale was included in the survey, then researchers need to decide how they want to analyze the data recorded for that scale. With some scales, items are thought to measure the same concept and may produce a total score. If scales are used and that information is included in the quantitative database, researchers may decide to group different aspects of those items from the scale together to obtain a composite score. Another option is running a Cronbach's alpha (Cronbach, 1951), which is a measure of the internal consistency of the scale and gives a sense of the validity and reliability of that particular scale as it relates to the sample (Grinnell & Unrau, 2014; Rosenthal, 2012; Thompson, 2001, 2002; Weinbach & Grinnell, 2009). Different sources offer suggestions for a "good" Cronbach's alpha, but overall a Cronbach's alpha of .60 or higher is sufficient.

Statistics that Determine Association

Statistics that determine association tells us if a relationship exists. The two statistical tests we discuss here are *chi-square* (χ^2) and *correlation* (r). Chi-square is used with nominal or ordinal levels of measurement and provides a measure of association based on *observed* (actual scores) and *expected* (statistically estimated) frequencies. With chi-square, the direction or strength of the relationship between the two variables is not specified. For example, chi-square tells us that something is there; we just do not know the strength of the relationship of that something. So naturally after running a chi-squared test and seeing that a relationship exists, researchers should run additional tests (e.g., a correlation) to learn about the strength of the relationship among those variables.

Correlation is typically used with interval and ratio levels of measurement. Correlation is a measure of association between two variables that also indicates *direction* (positive to negative) and *strength* of the relationship (–1.00 to +1.00). So correlation can give us what chi-square cannot. A correction (represented by "r") of zero means no relationship exists between the variables of interest, whereas an r of 1.00 indicates that a perfect relationship exists. A positive r value means there is a direct relationship, and a negative r value implies an inverse relationship between the two variables. Keep in mind that correlation still does not imply causation. Instead, we are able to understand the direction and the strength of the relationship between two variables.

We tend to use Pearson's r when running many of our correlations. This helps us address the question regarding how two interval- or

Table 4.6. Guide to Interpreting Correlations

Correlation	Interpreted as
Less than .20	Slight, almost negligible
.20 to .40	Low correlation; very weak relationship
.40 to .70	Moderate correlation; satisfactory relationship
.70 to .90	High correlation; noteworthy relationship
.90 to 1.00	Very high correlation; very strong relationship

ratio-level variables correlate. Correlations will range from 1 (positive) to –1 (negative or inverse). The way we interpret a positive correlation is as follows: The greater one variable, the greater the other. For example, consider the relationship between education and income. If our Pearson's r for this is .86, then we interpret this as the higher one's education, the higher one's income. A negative, or inverse, correlation tells us that the greater one variable, the less the other. For example, consider the relationship between life satisfaction and illness. If the Pearson's r for these variables is –.74, then we can safely assume that as life satisfaction goes up, the chance of illness goes down. Lack of correlation tells us that there is no relationship between the two variables. See Table 4.6 for suggestions for ways to interpret correlations in the quantitative results section of a mixed methods study.

We caution researchers to note that the use of r should not be confused with r^2, which is the *coefficient of determination*. This is the amount of variance in one variable explained by the other. For example, if we were to look at self-esteem and GPA, and the correlation for these two variables is $r = .60$, then the coefficient of determination is .36 ($.60^2$ or $.60 \times .60$). The way that we would interpret this is by stating the following: "Self-esteem explains 36% of the variance in GPA."

Statistics that Determine Differences

Statistics that determine differences are used to determine whether group differences exist for a specified variable. Based on the differences between two related groups, two unrelated groups, and more than two groups, specific tests are used (see Table 4.7). A dependent t test (also called a "paired t test" or a "paired samples t test") is used to compare the average values of characteristics measured on a continuous scale between two conditions of the same group, such as an assessment

Table 4.7. Statistics that Determine Differences

Type	Also known as	Used for	Questions answered/ Example
Dependent *t* test	Dependent samples *t* test, paired *t* test, or paired-samples *t* test	Two related groups; used to compare two sets of scores provided by one group of individuals; pretest and posttest scores	Are dependent samples different over time? / Are computer skills different for foster youth from pretest to posttest?
Independent *t* test	Independent samples *t* test	Two unrelated groups; used to compare two sets of scores, each provided by a different group of individuals	Do two independent samples belong to the same population? / Is there a difference in satisfaction between in-person and telephone interviews?
Analysis of variance	ANOVA	Used to compare three or more sets of scores, each provided by a different group of individuals	Do scores differ across groups? / Do attitudes about leadership style differ based on agency role (i.e., administrators, supervisors, direct service workers)?

between Time 1 compared to Time 2. The dependent *t* test can be used to evaluate depression scores, for example, measured on a continuous scale of a group involved in therapy at pretest (or before the intervention occurs) and posttest (or after the intervention has concluded).

An independent *t* test compares the average values of a characteristic measured on a continuous scale between two subgroups of a categorical variable. The independent *t* test is used to compare two sets of scores, each provided by a different group of individuals. For example, an independent *t* test can be used to measure differences in income measured in raw dollars by gender (defined in this case as either male or female). The reason this type of test is called "independent" is because the two subcategories in the categorical variable (i.e., male and female) are operationally defined to be mutually exclusive and mutually exhaustive. This means that everyone who participates in this study must fall into one of the two groups. So when testing mean differences under the independent *t* test, a question that can be asked is: Do two independent samples belong to the same population? For example, consider the question, "Is there a difference in preferences for in-person interviews compared to telephone interviews for the two groups under study?" If the answer to this question is "no," then we are determining that a difference does not exist between in-person and telephone interview preference with our male and female study participants.

Analysis of Variance

It may seem strange that a procedure used to compares means is called analysis of variance (ANOVA). However, this name was assigned to this type of analysis based on the fact that in order to test for statistical significance between means, we must actually use procedures that compare the variances. ANOVAs are used to compare three or more sets of scores, each provided by a different group of individuals. The purpose of an ANOVA is to test for significant differences between the means of these three or more groups. If an ANOVA is attempted with only two means, the results will produce the same results as the independent samples *t* test (if comparing two different groups of cases or observations) or the dependent *t* test (if comparing two variables in one set of cases or observations).

Multiple regression analysis helps estimate the value of a dependent variable based on the value of several independent variables. Multivariate statistics are "multi" due to the number of variables and the level of sophistication of understanding and interpretation researchers want to obtain from the analysis of those variables. Some other commonly used multivariate statistics include *factor analysis*, which examines the relationships among variables and reveals sets of variables (constructs that do or do not "hang" well together), and *structural equation modeling*, which is a method for testing theories about the relationships among variables.

Effect Sizes

Effect size can be used to estimate the true effect of the independent variable, to compare the results of one research project to the results of other projects, to help estimate the power of the statistic, and to help estimate the number of participants one needs in a study to maximize the chance of rejecting a false hypothesis (power). Reporting effect sizes provide readers with clear strengths of the associations between the variables reported.

Effect sizes take what we know about statistical significance to the next level by providing details about the magnitude of the difference between variables and/or groups (rather than just the fact that differences exist). Effect sizes can be characterized as small, medium, and large (Watkins et al., 2006). What these statistical terms mean numerically depends on the nature of the statistic being employed. They can be ascertained by looking at prior research findings, and in social/behavioral and health sciences research a medium effect is often assumed. Large effects are rare, and asserting a large effect must be well justified. We usually want the power of a test to be about .80 (80%) or higher.

The magnitude (or size) of the change is important with effect sizes and is not as valued with statistical significance testing (Kline, 2004; Thompson, 2006; Watkins et al., 2006). With the magnitude of effect sizes in mind, Jacob Cohen (1968) devised guidelines to address the first two questions. Over the years, we have found that authors emphasize the importance of interpreting effect sizes in relation to prior studies and do not simply use Cohen's benchmarks for what may be considered small, medium, and large effects. According to one of my (DCW) statistics professors from my doctoral program, Bruce Thompson (2001), "if people interpreted effect sizes [using fixed benchmarks] with the same rigidity that α = .05 has been used in statistical testing, we would merely be being stupid in another metric" (pp. 82–83). Kline (2004), on the other hand, supports the benchmarks but identifies cautions when interpreting the guidelines set by Cohen.

Answering the question "what is a substantive effect?" is a difficult task. According to Kline (2004), deciding whether an effect is important is complicated because expressing an effect's significance (i.e., theoretical, practical, or clinical) requires more discipline-specific expertise than when estimating its magnitude. Taking this into consideration, the answer depends on the research context. Each effect size reported is strongly related to the research question under investigation, such that a large effect may have as much substantive significance as a small effect. In most studies (i.e. intervention studies), a non-zero effect size is desired for the primary hypotheses. For example, if a social worker has designed a new juvenile justice program, his or her expectation is that the effect sizes will illustrate that the new program is more effective than traditional programs. On the other hand, if he or she is reviewing the unexpected consequences, or perhaps side effects of the new program, he or she will want near-zero effect sizes.

Vacha-Haase and Thompson (2004), in compliance with the American Psychological Association Task Force on Statistical Significance, suggested three guidelines for reporting effect sizes: (a) expressing what effect sizes are being reported, (b) interpreting the effect sizes by taking into consideration both their assumptions and their limitations, and (c) reporting confidence intervals for effect sizes and other study results. First, researchers must *state exactly what effect sizes are being reported*. Due to the numerous effect size choices, readers cannot accurately evaluate the effect if they do not know which effect size to interpret. Specifying the reported effect size also allows readers to convert the estimates so that they may be expressed in the same metrics. For example, if a reader is reviewing two articles, one in which the author reports Cohen's *d* and the other in which the author reports Pearson's *r*, he or she can convert both estimates to reflect either Cohen's *d* or Pearson's *r*. In this manner, "apples-to-apples" comparisons can be made (Vacha-Haase & Thompson, 2004).

Second, researchers should *interpret effect sizes by taking into consideration both their assumptions and their limitations*. When analytical assumptions are violated, the results and effect estimates are compromised (Vacha-Haase & Thompson, 2004). For example, when comparing effect size results across studies, researchers must consider differences in study designs. Effect sizes have a connection to the designs that they support, so acknowledging their differences is vital to understanding their estimates in relation to other studies. Among readers who desire to perform meta-analyses, reporting effect sizes will be especially useful. However, future researchers may choose to disregard a study that does not include effect sizes simply because they cannot find a comparable way to estimate the desired effect size results.

Third, researchers should *report confidence intervals for effect sizes and other study results*. Confidence intervals are easily modifiable to a graphical representation of the data, allowing a number of studies to be depicted efficiently (Thompson, 2002). As a highly recommended technique, the widths of confidence intervals can be compared to evaluate the precision of the estimates in a given study. Confidence intervals used to estimate a population value generally are symmetrical or nearly symmetric around a value. Due to their tendency to convey information about the precision of an estimated population value as well as statistical significance, confidence intervals are preferable to *p* values. Readers are strongly encouraged to view other resources (Thompson, 2002; Vacha-Haase & Thompson, 2004) for strategies used to construct and report confidence intervals.

Analyzing Data Using Statistical Software

SPSS (IBM Corp., 2013), SAS, and Stata are probably the most commonly used statistical software packages by social work researchers. We do not delve too deeply into the similarities and differences across these statistical software packages because this information exists elsewhere (e.g., Liu, 2009; Ward, 2013). However, we have used them all at some point over the course of our careers, and which one is most appropriate for each statistical analysis is a combination of personal preference and the statistical capabilities of each package. For example, we have found that when teaching statistics to social work students, SPSS is much more user-friendly because of the drop-down menus and the ease of clarity about which statistical tests a researcher may be running at any particular time. So for the purpose of teaching, we prefer SPSS; however, when it comes to running statistics for our own projects, we prefer Stata, as it allows for entering commands by hand and for most sophisticated analyses, such as the kind necessary to handle complex sample survey data. Despite the statistical package preferences described here, for the most part, many statistical software packages (SPSS, Stata, SAS, R, and Mplus) can perform similar techniques and produce the same results (Liu, 2009; Ward, 2013).

Thus far we have covered information about statistical tests that provide opportunities to describe our data and then infer our results to the general population. We have covered hypothesis testing, inference, correlation, effect sizes, and statistical power. It is beyond the scope of this pocket guide to provide advanced training on the procedures used to analyze quantitative data. Instead, we strive to provide enough of a foundation in both qualitative and quantitative data so that we can discuss this grounding in the context of mixed methods research in social work. For a more comprehensive description of statistical analysis techniques, we refer readers to resources produced by our colleagues (e.g., Grinnell & Unrau, 2014; Rosenthal, 2012; Rubin & Babbie, 2013; Onwuegbuzie & Combs, 2010; Weinbach & Grinnell, 2014), as well as other pocket guides in this series that cover social work–friendly statistical analyses (Cornelius & Harrington, 2014; Dattalo, 2008; Epstein, 2010; Orme & Combs-Orme, 2009; Randolph & Myers, 2013).

STEP 9:   INTERPRET THE INTEGRATED FINDINGS

Our final step for conducting mixed methods research in social work involves interpreting the findings of the mixed methods study. We maintain that integrating and interpreting the findings from a mixed methods study is much like interpreting the findings from a single-method study with one exception: mixed methods studies require consideration of the place where the qualitative and quantitative data come together, or integrate. This is also referred to as "mixing" the qualitative and quantitative methods (hence the term *mixed methods*). One of the biggest challenges faced by novice researchers interested in mixed methods is deciding how to integrate (and interpret the integration of) the findings from their mixed methods studies. In this section, we discuss ways to integrate qualitative and quantitative data.

Mixed methods scholars have suggested that there are several places (i.e., times) during the research process *when* data integration can occur (Bazeley, 2009; Bryman, 2006; Creswell, 2015; Fetters, Curry, & Creswell, 2013). Furthermore, data integration can also be organized by the different approaches (i.e., types) that are used to illustrate *how* the actual mixing of the qualitative and quantitative methods transpire. Two concepts are useful for understanding when and how mixing occurs: the type of mixing and the point of interface. The *type of mixing* is the way in which the quantitative and qualitative phases are integrated and interpreted. The *point of interface* is the time during which the quantitative and qualitative phases are mixed. In the following paragraphs we discuss four types of mixing strategies and four points of interface that can be used for data integration and interpretation of mixed methods studies.

TYPES OF MIXING: INTEGRATION AND INTERPRETATION

Creswell (2015) and others (Bazeley, 2009; Fetters et al., 2013; Maxwell & Loomis, 2003) have suggested that there are at least four types of integration of quantitative and qualitative data in a mixed methods study: merging the data, explaining the data, building the data, and embedding the data. Each is described below.

Merging the Data

Merging the data occurs at the end of a mixed methods study and involves bringing the qualitative and quantitative data together and comparing them. Integrating the data for the purpose of merging is probably one of the more popular integration techniques used by researchers new to mixed methods. This kind of data integration underscores the independent strengths of qualitative and quantitative approaches by allowing each to occur as single-method studies, with the goal of integrating the results of each single-method study after both are completed from beginning to end (Creswell, 2015; Creswell & Plano Clark, 2011; Kartalova-O'Doherty & Doherty, 2009). Data merging occurs most frequently with the convergent mixed methods design.

Explaining the Data

Integrating the data in a way that allows the researcher to provide an explanation for one of the methods applied is called integrating the data for the purposes of explaining. A useful example for this is the explanatory sequential design, which involves collecting and analyzing quantitative data first, then collecting and analyzing qualitative data for the purpose of explaining the results of the quantitative data. This is a way to provide what we have alluded to earlier in this text as a "voice behind the numbers" (Watkins, 2012) and may be particularly useful for social workers who are trying to develop some intervention strategies derived from Census data or other large sample survey data. In this example, social workers might analyze the large survey data set first, obtain results, then develop a focus group questionnaire (based on the findings from the large survey data) to gauge what members from a marginalized group think about the findings from the large survey. These qualitative data could then be used to frame a pilot intervention to improve the well-being of a marginalized group.

Building the Data

Integrating the data for the purposes of building involves using the qualitative results of a mixed methods study to build a quantitative phase of the study. This often occurs when researchers want to use the words of respondents to develop a new instrument, discover new variables, or generate a new intervention or characteristics of an intervention (Creswell, 2015). Integrating for the purpose of building most often occurs in an exploratory sequential design. With this type of design, words and concepts derived from the qualitative phase of the study can be translated into questions for a quantitative survey. This type of process is most useful to social work researchers who want to gauge the reaction of a larger sample to some of the findings from the smaller sample. Certainly developing a survey is not an easy task and involves working with experts in psychometrics to ensure that the question order, timing, layout, and wording are appropriate. But using qualitative data to help build the initial drafts of a survey is a useful strategy for social work researchers. Once a strong survey is developed, it can be tested for reliability and validity through repeated use and over time.

Embedding the Data

Integrating the data for the purposes of embedding involves using qualitative data to support the quantitative data, such as in a clinical or community-based experiment. Embedding occurs when data collection and analysis are linked at multiple points and is especially important in advanced intervention designs, but it can also occur in other designs (Creswell, 2015). Embedding may involve any combination of connecting, building, or merging, but the hallmark is recurrently linking qualitative data collection to quantitative data collection at multiple points (Fetters et al., 2013). A more common term for this kind of mixed methods data integration is a mixed methods intervention and/or evaluation program design. This type of data integration may seem more appropriate for social workers because it involves including an additional data component in an ongoing intervention that can help improve our understanding about a phenomenon of interest over time. An example might be studying a policy as it affects a particular constituency and checking in qualitatively with stakeholders throughout the rollout of the policy.

POINT OF INTERFACE: MIXING DATA AT DIFFERENT TIMES

Mixing is the explicit interrelating of a study's quantitative and qualitative phases. Deciding when to mix quantitative and qualitative phases of a mixed methods study is an important part of the data integration process. Creswell (2015) posits that the point of interface can occur during one of four times in a mixed methods study: during the design of the study, during data collection, during data analysis, and during data interpretation.

Mixing During the Design of the Study

When mixing during the design of a mixed methods study, the quantitative and qualitative phases are mixed during the larger design stage of the research process. Mixing at the design level can involve mixing with a traditional quantitative or qualitative research design, an emancipatory theory, a social science theory, or an overall program objective (Creswell, 2015). Thus, at the design level, it is likely one will gravitate toward one of three mixing strategies: embedded mixing, theoretical framework–based mixing, or program objective framework–based mixing. *Embedded mixing* involves embedding quantitative and qualitative methods within a design that is associated with one of these two methods (either quantitative or qualitative). When mixing within a *theoretical framework*, quantitative and qualitative phases are mixed within a transformative framework (such as feminism) or a substantive framework (such as social science theory). Regardless of which framework is used, each guides the entire study design. So, essentially, the methods and subsequent phases of the study are mixed using this theoretical perspective (Creswell, 2015). Mixing within a *program objective framework* involves mixing quantitative and qualitative phases within an overall program objective that guides the joining of multiple projects and studies within a multiphase project.

When mixing at the study design level, researchers should also consider how their findings will be interpreted based on the methodological framework used to guide the mixed methods study. For example, the transformative framework already evokes a certain social justice lens that is often used when working with marginalized groups. Thus, if researchers are fully immersed in a mixed methods study that uses the transformative framework as an overarching guide, then they will need to consider the way that social justice resonates throughout the study's conceptualization, data collection, data analysis, and dissemination phases. Regardless of which methodological framing is used for a mixed methods study (e.g., intersectionality, critical race theory, etc.), the framing should be applied to each step of the mixed methods process, especially during the data integration and interpretation stages.

Mixing During Data Collection

Mixing during data collection often involves collecting one set of data and then deciding to collect a second set of data (either quantitative or qualitative) to complete the study and meet the study objectives. When mixing during data collection we use a strategy called "connecting," whereby the result of one phase builds onto the data collection of the other phase. This connection occurs by using the results of the first phase to shape the collection of data for the second phase by specifying research questions, selecting participants, and developing data collection protocols or instruments based on what was found during the first phase of the study (Creswell, 2015). Mixing at the data collection level involves bringing the qualitative and quantitative phases of the mixed methods study together during the data collection phase. The most logical example is when we have a survey that contains both open-ended and closed-ended questions (Creswell, 2015; Grinnell & Unrau, 2014; Ulin et al., 2005). The closed-ended questions may offer some insight into a problem, but the open-ended questions may require additional data collection using focus groups or individual interviews that probe deeper into the problem under study.

Mixing During Data Analysis

Mixing during data analysis occurs when the quantitative and qualitative phases are analyzed together. Mixing at the data analysis level involves using the interactive strategy of "merging" to explicitly bring the two sets of results together through a combined analysis (Creswell, 2015). In other words, we would add an additional level of complexity to the project by first analyzing the quantitative and qualitative results separately and then further analyzing the quantitative and qualitative results collectively by relating them to each other in a matrix that facilitates comparisons and interpretations across and between the two data types. For example, if we are conducting a mixed method study using an explanatory sequential design, we would need to collect the quantitative data first, analyze that data, then make decisions about how we will analyze the qualitative data based on the results for the quantitative data. On the other hand, if we are conducting a mixed methods study using a convergent design, then the analysis, integration, and interpretation of the data will need to occur simultaneously.

Mixing During Data Interpretation

Mixing at the data interpretation level is probably the most common point of interface for researchers who are new to mixed methods. This is the point of mixing that involves drawing conclusions or inferences that reflect what was learned by combining the results from the quantitative and qualitative phases of the study (Creswell, 2015). This is often done by comparing or synthesizing the results in a discussion of the study findings. Creswell and Plano Clark (2011) suggest that all mixed methods designs should reflect on what was learned by the combination of methods in the final interpretation. For mixed methods designs that keep the two phases independent (such as the concurrent design), this is the only point in the research process where actual "mixing" occurs.

SUMMARY

This chapter has provided a streamlined process for how to prepare qualitative and quantitative data for analyses, how to analyze the data, and how to interpret the data using mixed methods approaches. Similar to the process of preparing data for single-method studies, the contribution of both qualitative and quantitative data to mixed methods studies does not elude the need to organize all aspects of the data collected and ensure that systematic steps in analyzing the data are performed. Mixed methods scholars have developed useful guidelines for preparing the data, organizing the data into concepts, developing the story, and maximizing rigor by validating conclusions. Despite this, however, one of the unique facets of mixed methods research is that it allows for flexible approaches within each data phase and at each step of the process. Hence mixed methods data collection, analysis, and interpretation may still be more of an art than a science. Therefore it remains imperative that social workers engaged in mixed methods research are able to interpret the findings of their projects and articulate the advantages of using mixed methods over a single method.

NOTE

1. We recommend the initial framework be established early; we are *not*, however, suggesting which concepts should be included—only the research team can decide which concepts are most relevant. We note this because instead of deciding in advance which concepts are important for a study, qualitative researchers tend to begin by recording verbatim what they hear or see during data analysis. This material is then reviewed to identify important concepts and their meaning for participants. These concepts are then refined throughout the coding and analysis process.

5

"Fifth Floor": Perils, Pitfalls, and Considerations

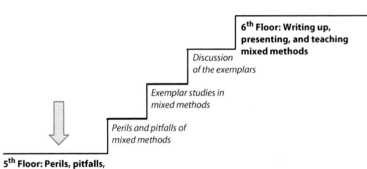

6th **Floor: Writing up, presenting, and teaching mixed methods**

Discussion of the exemplars

Exemplar studies in mixed methods

Perils and pitfalls of mixed methods

5th **Floor: Perils, pitfalls, and considerations**

This chapter presents some of the "messy" elements of mixed methods research to help readers avoid potential mishaps as they work through their mixed methods projects. We use our own mixed methods research experience as a backdrop to our description of the perils and pitfalls that we have experienced over the years. In this chapter we also provide a synthesis of three exemplar mixed methods studies that will help provide an understanding of the range of integration types (and integration depth) that can occur across studies. One goal of the chapter is to get social work researchers excited and not intimidated about the breadth and complexity of these studies—opening up new windows of possibilities and once again inviting them to think about their own research from this mixed point of view. We begin with a brief discussion of the ethical considerations of social work in relation to the framing of mixed methods research.

ETHICAL CONSIDERATIONS IN SOCIAL WORK RESEARCH

As social workers who engage in mixed methods research, it is important for us to consider some of the challenges that we may face. To some degree, the same challenges that we face conducting single-method studies will also be true for our mixed methods study. Therefore we should be keenly aware of these challenges and anticipate ethical ways to address them. First, however, let us first define ethics. *Ethics* is defined as proper and improper behavior regarding moral duty and obligation. At its core, ethics is associated with morality, and both deal with matters of right and wrong. Ethical behavior in social work research and practice implies that social workers will uphold the moral obligation or duty to act in a way that is consonant with their professional values (National Association of Social Workers, 2014).

Ethical issues in mixed methods research by social workers can arise from several aspects of research, such as the kinds of problems social workers want to investigate, the methods or procedures used to collect valid and reliable data, exposure to conditions that may involve some harm to subjects, the research settings, the people social workers serve, and sensitive data. The purpose of ethical principles and guidelines in social work is to help protect clients, subjects, or respondents; delineate professional responsibilities; direct data gathering; and guide change effort toward acceptable and worthwhile goals. The National Association of Social Workers' (2014) Code of Ethics includes statements about the ethical conduct and reporting of research. Namely, when it comes to scholarship and research, the social worker should be guided by the conventions of scholarly inquiry. (See Table 5.1.) For a more detailed description of ethical considerations in single-method

Table 5.1. Ethics in Social Work Research

- The social worker engaged in research should
  - Consider carefully its *possible consequences for human beings.*
  - Ascertain that the *consent of participants in the research is voluntary and informed,* without any implied deprivation or penalty for refusal to participate and with due regard for participants' privacy and dignity. If the study features ethnography or a longitudinal embedded design, consent may need to be reviewed with each level of contact that is made with the participants.
  - Protect *participants from unwarranted physical or mental discomfort,* distress, harm, danger, or deprivation. In other words, end the session if the participant is not able to continue with the interview. Also, have a plan in the event that a research participant needs to be referred to a health or human services professional, should the research bring up uncomfortable emotions.
- The social worker who engages in the evaluation of services or cases should discuss them *only* for professional purposes and *only with persons directly and professionally concerned with them.*
- Information obtained about participants in research should be treated as *confidential.* Though it is difficult to promise complete confidentiality due to possible unforeseen circumstances, social workers should use language in the consent that suggests that every precaution to safeguard participants' information will be taken.

and mixed methods research, see other resources where our colleagues elaborate on these social work ethics (Antle & Regehr, 2003; Bisman, 2004; Landau, 2008; Peled & Leichtentritt, 2002; Reamer, 2013; Thyer, 2009, 2011). We encourage readers to refer to these sources for information on social work research ethics, both in general and with regard to qualitative and quantitative methods.

PERILS AND PITFALLS OF MIXED METHODS

Mixed methods research is not unlike other research in that there are certain advantages and disadvantages that should be taken into consideration. Here we caution readers about 11 of the most common pitfalls among novice mixed methods researchers: (1) misjudging one's skill level (e.g., what one can and cannot do); (2) assembling the wrong team; (3) not reviewing the literature on the topic; (4) not working through the mixed methods research design forward and backward; (5) not preparing for the worse; (6) not thinking ahead to the final report; (7) not sticking to the plan (as much as possible); (8) not enjoying every moment; (9) not considering the audience; (10) not showing how mixed methods helps to address the problem; and (11) not providing a visual depiction of the mixed methods study. We discuss each of these next.

Misjudging One's Skill Level

We totally get it: most researchers believe they are completely capable of taking on the tasks (and various stages) involved in conducting a mixed methods study. However, planning a mixed methods study is the wrong time to be overly confident in one's abilities or to convince oneself that now is the best time to "finally learn that new method." This false sense of confidence and capabilities can result in a bad experience for researchers and their teams (not to mention the research participants). Instead, we encourage readers to focus on the skills that they *do* have and what they *do* bring to the table. If a person is not proficient in both qualitative and quantitative methods, perhaps he or she is fairly skilled at single-method research (either quantitative or qualitative methods). Or perhaps a person is not skilled in methods at all but has a keen eye for identifying and framing the research question that needs to be explored by a mixed methods team, or can help locate an array of talented team members who possess the skills to help get the job done. Regardless of the case, being honest with oneself and about one's capabilities is vital. Researchers can then act responsibly on behalf of the communities they want to help and convene a team of people who bring unique talents and experiences to a mixed methods study, so that each phase of the study is performed by competent team members. Doing this benefits the project, the researcher, the research participants—and the funders!

Assembling the Wrong Team

Remember that mixed methods studies require multiple inputs of expertise and effort (Curry & Nunez-Smith, 2015; Padgett, 2009). Therefore researchers should avoid assembling a team of colleagues who do not bring certain necessary strengths to the mixed methods project. In other words, creating a mixed methods team that consists of colleagues with whom one enjoys working may make work on the project enjoyable, but it may not help achieve the study goals or meet the program objectives. Instead, we suggest researchers assemble a team of people who have the skills necessary to complete the work. If they are not sure which colleagues should be invited to join the team, researchers should consult with mentors, supervisors, and other colleagues about their skill levels; request evidence that demonstrates their abilities (such as an internal report or published work); and find a time to meet with them to gauge their interest in the project and to see if they would be a good fit for the team.

It is also important to gauge the number of consultants, or "advisers," needed for the project, as well as the number of "workers." There is a distinction. Advisers provide consultation and advice on certain aspects of the project through the various steps of the mixed methods study. These advisers most likely will not, however, engage in the day-to-day study activities; that is the job of the workers. Oftentimes workers are people hired specifically for the project, or they may be students or interns who desire social work research experience. Workers are the project team members who can provide status updates on the various phases of the project and operationalize the research directions provided by the leadership and through consultation with the advisers.

Not Reviewing the Literature

Mixed methods studies are not unlike other research studies in that they are an iterative research process. This iteration usually involves posing research questions that are answered, but then the answers to these questions raise ideas about other questions that need to be answered. Given this, it is always a good idea to review the literature on a topic (prior to beginning a study) to see what kinds of research have been conducted on the topic. Also, when reviewing this literature, one should pay close attention to the methodology and methods used in the research. For example, if all previous references are either quantitative or qualitative, this could provide the rationale for exploring a missing component of the literature using a mixed methods approach. As simple as this may seem, many social work researchers do not do this very important step in the research process and instead depend on their clinical experience or agency traditions (Grinnell & Unrau, 2014) to make decisions about how they will move forward with a research project.

Thus, social workers who want to conduct a mixed methods study should first do a thorough search for peer-reviewed (scientific) journal articles about the phenomenon of interest. Oftentimes these articles can clue one in to the current gaps in the knowledge about the topic and thereby provide an area of focus for current and future inquiry. Also, these journal articles can help provide information on how the topic has been investigated in the past, which methods were used, and the success (or failure) of those methods in helping to address the topic (and answer the subsequent research questions). Why recreate the wheel and/or make the same mistakes that someone else has made? That would be a waste of time and resources, and supervisors (and funders) will be very pleased that this major pitfall was avoided.

Not Working Through the Design—Forward and Backward

When planning for a mixed methods study (or any study for that matter), it is very important to work through the research plan, forward and backward. One of the things we tend to do when we are planning for our mixed methods studies is we sketch out a draft design of the study. This sketch is usually very rough at the earlier stages of the planning process (and may even be on a Post-It note, a napkin, or a legal pad), but as the ideas begin to crystalize, we eventually recreate the drawing on our computer (using a program like Microsoft Word or PowerPoint), then polish the design throughout the duration of the mixed methods study.

As researchers work through a study design, forward and backward, we encourage them to talk through it (aloud). It may even be helpful to try to explain it to someone who does not know anything about research (or mixed methods). A researcher can also print out a copy of the design, hand it to a colleague (or significant other), and see if it makes sense to them. This may seem like a lot of work during the planning stages of a mixed methods study, but taking steps like this to work out the "kinks" during the planning stages of a study saves time later in the process. The mixed methods design (and the process for the study) must be easy to understand and clear to all current and potential stakeholders. We have found that working through the design forward and backward during the planning stages of a mixed methods studies has grossly reduced the amount of work that we need to do on the backend of the study.

Not Preparing for the Worse

We suppose others would call this "have a backup plan," but we prefer to call it "not preparing for the worse." We like focusing on preparing for the worse because, in our opinion, having a backup plan implies a complete overhaul and reworking of the original plan, whereas preparing for the worse allows us to address certain challenges that we anticipate may occur at different phases of the mixed methods study. A useful strategy that has worked for us is making a list of "*If . . . then . . .*" statements that relate directly to various aspects of our study. For example, to prepare for the worse for recruitment for a mixed methods study, one of the statements could be "*If* we cannot recruit a sufficient number of study participants during the 2-week recruitment period, *then* we will expand our recruitment locations to include churches and local athletic facilities."

Another statement could be "*If* our recruited participants turn out to be ineligible for the study, *then* we will ask them to provide names of other potential participants we can invite to participate in our study (i.e., snowball sampling)." The reason this strategy is helpful is, rather than anticipating a complete reworking of a study, researchers can anticipate potential steps that may present challenges and already have a list of alternate strategies that can help them overcome these challenges. From a logistical perspective, this technique focuses on the challenge, isolates it, and allows one to prepare for the worst-case scenario regarding that specific aspect of the study. Depending on the study, researchers may choose to create two or more "*If . . . then . . .*" statements so that during their (potential) moment of panic, they have a safety net.

Not Thinking Ahead to the Final Report

Although this is a pitfall that may appear counterintuitive, social work researchers who do not think ahead to the final report when planning for their mixed methods studies will be doing themselves a huge disservice.

As difficult as this may seem, it is helpful to try to imagine what a mixed methods final report will look like during the planning stages. That way researchers can determine which aspects of the study will be essential to the final report and be sure to include them in the study. This tip is particularly helpful for those of us who conduct mixed methods research with the support of grants and other funding resources. Thinking ahead to the final report during the planning stages of a mixed methods study can also help the research team remain focused during potential times of distraction and disruption as they proceed through the various steps of the mixed methods research process.

Not Sticking to the Plan (As Much as Possible)

The beauty of social work research is that it often allows one to interact with diverse people who have interesting experiences that they want to share. This is why many of us chose social work as a profession in the first place. However, while this may have been our motivation for becoming social workers, this feeling needs to be managed throughout our social work careers, and especially when conducting mixed methods research. We note this because sometimes our personal interests can pull us away from our research interests, resulting in a deviation from the original plan. As social work researchers (often employed by agencies and supported by external funding), this can be a bad situation. Researchers do not want to become like Alice in Wonderland and find themselves falling further and further down the rabbit hole of personal interests. Instead, when conducting a mixed methods study, researchers should try to stick to the original plan as much as possible.

A helpful practice that we have developed over the years is to journal during each stage of our mixed methods study. This is particularly helpful for those of us whose minds tend to wander when we encounter interesting data. A way to avoid becoming distracted is to keep a diary or a journal about the data, make notes about what interesting aspect of the data should be revisited in the near future, and then proceed with the original study as planned. That way the research team's time, energy, and resources can be directed toward the matter at hand (the current mixed methods study), but interesting data can be returned to at some point. Another helpful practice is to write research aims/questions/

hypotheses for the current mixed methods study on Post-It notes and stick them on computer monitors or other places where they can be viewed regularly. This practice helps prevent us from straying too far from our original intent for the study.

Not Enjoying the Mixed Methods Study

Sometimes when we are in the middle of a study (whether it is a pilot study or the fifth iteration of an intervention), we forget to enjoy the moment and take it all in. Unfortunately, many of us have an "I'll be glad when it's over approach" to research, instead of relishing in the success of having a study active and ongoing. Think of it this way instead: "My work is exciting, and many people will never have the opportunity that I have to collect important information to answer a research question and improve the living and working conditions of this particular group of people." Likewise, engagement in such work is important to the people being helped and to the social work profession overall. Do not forget this pearl of wisdom as potential challenges arise during the research process. In most cases, if researchers come across a challenge that they cannot handle, they should have access to resources that can help them.

Not Considering the Audience

When giving a presentation of any kind, it is important to always consider the audience. Depending on the competency level of that audience, modifications may need to be made to a presentation to ensure that the content presented is clear and appropriate. This is especially true when writing up and presenting mixed methods findings. For example, if one is presenting to a crowd of experts, certain aspects of the mixed methods procedures can be excluded. However, if presenting to an audience who has little to no familiarity with mixed methods (which is usually the case during this current era in the history of mixed methods), enough resources, background references, materials, and sources need to be provided so that the audience can receive the information in a language and style that is clear to them and in a context that they can apply to their own knowledge base. The most embarrassing place a presenter can find himself (or herself) is presenting his or her mixed methods findings to an audience who either knows too little or knows more than the presenter. It is also a good idea to have some ideas about ways to modify the mixed methods presentation (on the spot, if needed) so as to be prepared for the unanticipated audience member who may truly have no prior knowledge of mixed methods or even the audience member who has written three or four books on the topic.

Not Showing How Mixed Methods Help to Address the Problem

One of the stickiest situations one may encounter is to be standing in front of an audience of colleagues presenting a mixed methods research and to not know the answer to a very important question that is frequently asked during mixed methods presentations: "Why did you decide to use mixed methods approaches for this project?" "Couldn't you have just used a survey (or in-depth interview) to capture the same kind of data?" We raise this point because it is important to not only know the ins and outs of mixed methods for the purpose of the research but also to be able to articulate why the use of mixed methods is an advantage, over and above a single method, for your project. Although it is clear that one has more data with mixed methods than with one method alone, mixed methods researchers must be resourceful in using the data they obtain in a meaningful way. Therefore, consider what mixed methods adds to our knowledge base and be prepared to articulate this in a clear and concise way, whenever necessary.

Not Providing a Visual Representation of the Study

Visual representations of a mixed methods study are valuable tools that can help communicate the mixed methods design, procedures, and findings. (We discuss this more in chapter 6.) Not providing a visual representation of a mixed methods study while writing up and presenting the mixed methods research can do more harm than good, especially given the complex nature of some mixed methods studies. Most studies need some type of diagram or graph to help explain the study procedures to the audience. Other visual methods, such as photographs, word clouds, and maps, can also enrich the findings considerably. We elaborate on visual representations and the types of diagrams used for mixed methods research more in chapter 6.

Now that we have covered some of the perils and pitfalls associated with mixed methods research, we now transition into a consideration that we believe can help reduce the likelihood of running into the messiness of mixed methods studies: reviewing mixed methods studies from the peer-reviewed literature.

CONSIDERATIONS: EXEMPLAR MIXED METHODS STUDIES IN SOCIAL WORK

In this section we highlight three mixed methods studies and provide our own annotations about each study, as well as some insights regarding the studies presented. Our rationale for reviewing these mixed methods studies is to guide the reader through our interpretation of some real-world data and provide a glimpse into each research team's thought processes. We were also inspired by an article that described the benefits and challenges of mixed methods for investigating the reduction of health disparities (Stewart, Makwarimba, Barnfather, Letourneau, & Neufeld, 2008) and thought we might be able to apply some of the authors' strategies to social work studies organized loosely around some of the issues faced by professionals in social work. Although we have opted to rank these studies based on their levels of data integration, in no way does defining a study as "low" or "high" speak to the quality of the study itself or the findings. Rather, we have chosen this language as a way to designate the *level of integration* (i.e., actual "mixing" of the methods) for each study. Each of these studies underwent its own peer-reviewed process, were all accepted for publication, and were published in top tier journals, thereby speaking to the quality of each study's topic, methods, and writing.

Two of the exemplar studies were reviewed are social work studies, and the third was selected from the allied field of family medicine. This study is slightly older than the social work studies, perhaps displaying that other disciplines have been utilizing these designs and methods more confidently and longer than social work has. The fact that the word *integration* was used in the study's title raised our curiosity as to how this kind of framing would be demonstrated in a study about mental health. This study was also chosen because one of the co-authors, Dr. Joseph Gallo, regularly co-teaches mixed methods workshops with Dr. John W. Creswell, and because appropriate integration can serve as a model for social work as we design and implement our mixed methods studies.

Exemplar Study 1 (Social Work): Low Level of Integration

Teasley, M., Canfield, J. P., Archuleta, A. J., Crutchfield, J., & McCullough Chavis, A. (2012). Perceived barriers and facilitators to school social work practice: A mixed methods study. *Children & Schools, 34*(3), 145–153.

Understanding barriers to practice is a growing trend in school social work research, as some of these barriers may be sociocultural, economic, environmental, personal, systemic, or institutional by nature (Adelman & Taylor, 2002, 2005). Schools, through their teachers and administrators, carry out their mission and become the main facilitators of evidence-based practices. The basis of the study by Teasley, Canfield, Archuleta, Crutchfield, and McCullough Chavis (2012) is that utilizing qualitative and quantitative methods is necessary to identify and document the factors that inhibit or advance the multitude of services in which school social workers engage. It was important to the researchers that they explore barriers and facilitators in different geographic locations to understand the needs of regional service areas and compare and contrast these differences.

Methods

In this Institutional Review Board–approved, concurrent nested mixed methods study, two types of data were collected simultaneously. A 115-item instrument was developed for this study, which contained (in addition to demographic and other information) 16 quantitative and 2 qualitative items that had been developed based on the findings from prior studies by Teasley and colleagues (2012). The 16 quantitative items were placed on a 5-point Likert scale and the 2 qualitative items (placed at the end of the survey) prompted participants to respond to the following solicitations: "In your opinion, and in order of importance, please list barriers to your school social work practice" and "In your opinion, and in order of importance, please list what facilitates your social work practice."

Respondents were 282 out of the 585 attendees at a school social work conference in the Midwest who agreed to complete the survey.

According to the sample demographics table, the majority of respondents possessed master's degrees in social work, with an average of 8.99 years working as a school social worker. The majority of respondents identified as White, female, and situated in a suburban area; only 7% of the sample identified as being located in an inner city. Respondents were compensated by receiving entry into a drawing for one of two cash prizes, and the data collection was completed after the second conference day.

Data Analysis

Qualitative and quantitative data were collected simultaneously but analyzed separately. Statistical analyses were conducted on the 16 Likert scale items to test several relationships. The 16 items developed by the researchers explored such constructs as time constraints, bureaucracy, resources, staffing, motivation, and burnout (for a full list see Teasley et al., 2012). Mean score, standard error, and standard deviation were derived for each item. Bivariate analyses were conducted by creating a barrier to practice composite variable and examining this score with some of the demographic data collected.

The authors performed a content analysis on the two qualitative items mentioned previously that utilized two reviewers who created separate lists of barriers and facilitators mentioned by the respondents. The separate lists were then combined to create a master list of categories, and then reviewers returned to their lists to begin the process of seeing how their individual lists mapped onto the master list. The researchers used two methods to measure their interrater reliability (for details see Teasley et al., 2012) and noted that across several categories perfect agreement between the reviewers existed. The data generated from the qualitative phase of this study was the kappa score agreement for their categories. A table of the agreement between the reviewers is provided in the article.

Key Findings

Findings were separated into two categories: perceived barriers and perceived facilitators. The perceived barriers with the highest mean scores were time limitations, followed by staffing and caseloads. The authors cite these findings as consistent with their prior studies. The perceived facilitators were collaboration, communication, cooperation, and attitudes of the school staff and was the highest-ranking item in the qualitative ranking. Other strong facilitators were knowledge aware-ness and training and parents and family, rounding out the top three ranked items.

Insights and Reflections on the Use of Mixed Methods

The use of a survey that has both quantitative and a few open-ended qualitative items is often an early point of entry for a mixed methods research team. This type of design is frequently used by researchers pri-marily trained in quantitative methods who are beginning to see the value of qualitative data and who want to begin including items in their surveys that can help address some of the more contextual aspects of their research questions. This design's focus on the interrater reliability is within the comfort zone of quantitative researchers (as well as those researchers who are new to mixed methods), but it is not a necessary element for a mixed methods study.

In the limitations section of the study, the researchers state that there was not equal development of the barriers and facilitators ques-tion and almost all of the items were constructed to yield the per-ceptions of school barriers, with only the qualitative item for the facilitators. Similarly, the study did not return to a discussion of the nested design in the data analysis. This was perhaps the study's big-gest weakness and leaves the reader unclear about how the mixed methods design was operationalized, as well as the strengths of the mixed methods design over use of a single-method design to answer the research question.

Though the article had many strengths, there was no push to inte-grate the findings except in the reader's understanding of the two data displays. While a researcher can certainly use multiple forms of written data in a mixed methods study, the chance for contextualization and reflection on the quantitative findings by the respondent is minimized with this type of study. It is, however, an interesting means for generat-ing hypotheses for future quantitative studies or developing an inter-view guide for future qualitative studies.

Exemplar Study 2 (Social Work): Moderate Level of Integration

Haight, W., Kayama, M., Kincaid, T., Evans, K., & Kim, N. K. (2013). The elementary-school functioning of children with maltreatment histories and mild cognitive or behavioral disabilities: A mixed methods inquiry. *Children and Youth Services Review, 35,* 420–428.

This mixed methods inquiry examined the school functioning of elementary school–age children with maltreatment histories and mild cognitive or behavioral disabilities (Haight, Kayama, Kincaid, Evans, & Kim, 2013). The researchers contend that in order to design effective school interventions that support the child who has a maltreatment history, one must use both quantitative and qualitative methods to explore these important constructs. The article begins with a literature review of studies that demonstrate the co-occurrence of disability and maltreatment. When out-of-home care is added as a variable, the rates of children identified with learning disabilities and maltreatment appear to be reciprocally related and affect school functioning at an alarming rate. In this study the researchers focused on the school functioning of children with maltreatment histories who had mild disabilities of cognition and behavior and used qualitative and quantitative data to address four research questions:

1. To what extent are children with mild cognitive or behavioral disability in the geographic area explored also represented in child protective services?
2. What is the academic achievement of these children compared to children with maltreatment issues who do not have disabilities?
3. What strengths and challenges to school functioning do professionals describe for these children and their families?
4. How do professionals describe cross-system collaborations in supporting these children and their families?

Methods
The quantitative study tied to the first two research questions consisted of gaining access to state child protective administrative data to identify the children with maltreatment and disability histories. This database also provided information about the children's academic achievements. The sample consisted of 10,394 elementary students in public schools in two Minnesota counties. The parameters for the examination were between the years 2009 and 2010 and included third through sixth graders with substantiated abuse in their files. The cognitive and behavioral

history was determined through Individual Education Plans and enrollment in special education. If children were receiving these services because of physical impairments, including hearing and vision loss, they were excluded. Although the literature suggested a strong linkage with out-of-home placement, this sample found only 5.6% of the children had out-of-home placements. A slight majority of this sample was male and White (52% and 54%, respectively).

The qualitative phase of the study, which addressed research questions 3 and 4, utilized face-to-face semistructured interviews with 22 child welfare professionals and 15 educators. Interviews were audiotape-recorded and lasted 30 to 60 minutes. Respondents (of which 73% were female) were asked to describe two illustrative cases and to comment on collaboration between service providers involved in cases of child maltreatment cases in which the child had a cognitive or behavioral disability. The interviews were transcribed verbatim and then coded by two independent researchers. Disagreements were resolved through discussions by the research team. Methods of credibility and rigor were mentioned but not discussed in detail.

Data Analysis

It appears that quantitative and qualitative data were analyzed separately and then reported according to the questions that were tagged to that method. Question 1 was a report of the demographics of the sample, including percentages found in the diagnostic categories of cognitive or behavioral disability. Question 2 was about academic achievement and was addressed using analysis of variance to analyze the reading and math scores. Overall the reading scores declined as the grade level increased, but the effect size was small. The math scores also declined as grade levels increased, and the effect size was small as well. A serendipitous finding involved the number of tardies and/or absences from school. The children examined missed more days per year than their peers who did not have cognitive/behavioral disabilities and maltreatment issues. The effect sizes for the analysis of these data were also small.

Key Findings

The quantitative findings were mapped by grade using mean scores, but (as noted previously) despite the large sample, the effect sizes were small. The study was not hypothesis driven for the quantitative data;

rather, research questions were asked and trends were noted. The qualitative data provided a different narrative of the experience, and included data from professionals who were fully engaged in service settings with children with this constellation of needs. The first strong endorsement by professionals was around the description of multiple, complex unmet basic and mental health needs. More than 76% of the professionals interviewed discussed unmet needs, which also included trauma and loss, and noted the impediment to learning that these unmet needs yielded. They went on to discuss not only students' unmet needs but the parents' or caregivers' difficulties and how those contributed to the type of support they were able to provide to the child.

The third research question was addressed by a majority of the professionals, and their responses alluded to their inability to provide timely and appropriate interventions to these children because some of the challenges faced by the children were either masked or not properly identified, creating difficulties for those who work with them. A second important reflection by the professionals regarding the children with positive outcomes was the protective factor created by having a positive engagement with school—whether the child, family, or both. Findings from the interviews that were related to the fourth research question on cross-systems collaboration first gave the respondents a chance to weigh in on the importance of cross-systems collaboration in their work with children and families. Seventy-three percent said that the communication they witnessed was inadequate and needed to be improved. Another criticism in this section concerned the fact that the systems that they helped to create and were working in were not friendly to the families they served, nor was there much assistance to help families to navigate through the system.

Insights and Reflections on the Use of Mixed Methods

An underlying aim for the authors of the study was to examine disorders that are relatively hidden (e.g., learning difficulties) and how those may be a predictor and an outcome of child maltreatment. They also noted something that they were surely already aware of in their practice: when the households are chaotic, a hidden disability seems to disappear if there was someone who could intervene to help assist the child with better school functioning. Noticing this web of interrelated circumstances caused the researchers to call for a holistic approach in assessment, screening, engagement of adult caretakers, and implement-ing better cross-systems approaches by the professionals for the benefit of the child.

In the mixed methods design, the researchers noted that adminis-trative data were not collected for research purposes and so they were not able to examine all that they wanted to in regard to their questions. Looking specifically at math and reading scores was useful but limited in that it gave only a small glimpse into the larger issues related to school functioning for the children in these counties. As the authors note, an ability to incorporate interviews of some of the children and parents would have provided more data to triangulate and created more rich layers through which to examine this important topic.

The emphasis of the article was clearly on the qualitative data, and the purpose of the design was to amplify the interrelated parts of the phenomena and provide a holistic picture. In this regard, the authors were successful. They did not name their design beyond this desire to amplify, and integration was not a strong emphasis in this mixed methods study. It seems that if the researchers had used their own county-wide survey, they would have had more ability to integrate and converge the findings.

Exemplar Study 3 (Family Medicine): High Level of Integration

Wittink, M. N., Barg, F. K., & Gallo, J. J. (2006). Unwritten rules of talk-ing to doctors about depression: Integrating qualitative and quantitative methods. *Annals of Family Medicine, 4*(4), 302–308.

The primary health care setting is a place in which older adults receive treatment for depression and other mental health concerns, since they do not usually find themselves in the specialty mental health care settings. Despite this, many studies alert us to the fact that these adults are often not diagnosed properly, nor do patients receive the best treatment for their presenting mental health problem. Comfortable relationships and com-munications with one's primary-care doctor do seem to be the basis for improvement in diagnosis and treatment, but the patients themselves are often left to initiate these discussions. This study focuses on patients' views of the interactions with their physicians and is based on an integrated mixed methods design. The study differs from other studies that have explored patients' views in that it allowed patients to reflect on numerous aspects of their encounters with the physician over time in order to gain a glimpse into the communication patterns between a doctor and a patient, specifically when the patient has a diagnosis of depression.

Methods

This article reports the findings from a substudy of a larger project called the Spectrum Study. The parent study was a cross-sectional survey of patients 65 and over who were receiving care at nonacademic primary-care sites (n = 355). The substudy included 48 individuals. The measurement strategies included a physician rating of the patient at the visit, two well-known depression inventories (the Center for Epidemiologic Studies, Depression and the Beck Anxiety Inventory). The authors also used the Beck Hopelessness Scale, a medical comorbidity scale, and a health outcomes short form survey, and they assessed cognition with the mini mental status exam. Semistructured interviews, which were conducted in the patients' homes, were transcribed and coded. The interview questions were focused on the patients' perceptions of their encounters with their physicians. A sample of the questions showed that there was an algorithm-style format to the guide, meaning if they answered yes to an item, there were additional questions to probe for content related to the response.

Data Analysis

The study was both hypothesis-testing and hypothesis-generating, and the two phases of qualitative and quantitative data were woven together for the analysis. Qualitative and quantitative data were collected at the same point in time from the patients. In the first phase the researchers compared the personal characteristics of patients who identified themselves as being depressed while their physicians did not. The authors used t tests and a statistical significance level set at .05. In the second phase of analysis they used the constant comparative method, moving between the codes and text iteratively to derive themes related to patients' talking with their physicians. This is a grounded theory data analysis strategy used to compare one piece of data (one theme) to all other pieces of data to develop conceptualizations of the possible relations between various pieces of data. During this phase, the researchers did not have access to the survey data.

Key Findings

Fifty-three patients from the 102 who participated in the interviews reported being depressed. Five of the transcripts were not used due to missing data, leaving 48 in the final analysis. Physicians rated 27 of these patients as depressed, with missing diagnosis on 21 of those patients in the sample. There were no significant differences between the two groups that the physicians rated on any characteristic, except for age. The mean age of the patient rated by the physician was 73, and the mean age of the patient rated by the physician as not depressed was 77. The four qualitative themes—which were identified in the narratives of patients describing the relationship with their doctor—included the following: (a) "My doctor just picked it up" (patients describe that physicians acknowledged the depression without them being explicit about it); (b) "I'm a good patient" (this theme emerged from the data as patients described that they feel liked by their physician); (c) "They just check out your heart and things" (this data came from patients who described that physicians attend to the physical and ignore the emotional); and (d) "They'll just send you to a psychiatrist" (this was described by patients who felt that if they brought up emotional content they would get a psychiatric referral).

The integrated data analysis occurred in table form—as the characteristics of the patients were matched to the themes—and noted whether physicians had rated the individual as depressed. The results of the integrated findings are as follows: all of the patients who discussed the theme "my doctor just picked it up" were women; only 3 out of 8 patients who thought they were good patients were rated by their doctor as depressed; patients who brought up the theme of the doctor focusing on physical rather than emotional factors tended to have more education and were White; and all of the patients who brought up being referred to a psychiatrist were rated by their physician as depressed.

Insights and Reflections on the Use of Mixed Methods

Limitations as described by the authors included using patient perceptions of their encounters with their physicians, as well as patient self-report of depression versus chart review. The quantitative data were used to "sharpen the ability to distinguish themes among participants." The authors went on to reflect on the findings in each of their themes in ways that are very enlightening for the reader and offered alternative possibilities for generating hypotheses. The authors realized if they had limited their findings to the quantitative measures they would have missed all the data related to the patient's perspective, which helped to contextualize the study and pushed the findings to the next logical place they would want to explore. It is possible that this clear and meaningful study might have been enhanced by triangulating other sources of data (i.e., chart review) and adding observation of patient/physician encounters to the data sources. A longitudinal view, which may or may not have included ethnographic methods, might have honed the data even further, providing more rigor to the research.

DISCUSSION OF THE EXEMPLARS

Reviewing these three exemplar studies in this order was intentional, as we presented these exemplars in the order for how the qualitative and quantitative data were integrated: from low to medium to high, based on our mixed methods review criteria. We encourage readers to note that each study provides a different level of integration for the qualitative and quantitative methods and data used. Some readers may feel that the Teasley et al. (2012) study is not a "pure" mixed methods study due to the lower level of integration used. Nevertheless, it is important to note that the way in which this exemplar study was conducted and reported is quite common in mixed methods reports. While we value the contribution that this exemplar study makes to the science of mixed methods (hence our decision to include it as an "exemplar" in this text), we would have liked to see the authors move toward more data integration. In our review of these three exemplar studies, we would posit that the Haight et al. (2013) study is definitely a mixed methods study without "true" integration—in other words, a mixed methods study that separates the data collection from the data analysis steps. We believe that there was an opportunity for true integration here, but the authors did not capitalize on it. In contrast, we found the Wittink et al. (2006) study to be a wonderful example for how integration can occur and deemed this study at the "high" level of our mixed methods data integration continuum.

SUMMARY

All research studies are met with challenges, and mixed methods research is no exception. Oftentimes the complex nature of mixed methods design, data collection, and data analysis and integration can present unforeseen challenges that may be less likely to occur during studies that use single methods (i.e., either qualitative *or* quantitative). Therefore, in an effort to avoid potential mishaps by researchers as they work through their mixed methods projects, we have used this chapter to outline the perils and pitfalls that we have experienced in our own mixed methods work over the years. Although we are certain that other pitfalls exist, our hope is that this chapter will provide a foundation for some of the challenges that should be anticipated by social workers who engage in mixed methods research. Our synthesis of the exemplar mixed methods studies should provide an understanding of the range of integration types (and integration depth) that can occur across mixed methods studies. Thereby we offer models we hope readers will consider using as resources to frame their future mixed methods projects.

6

"Sixth Floor": Writing Up, Presenting, and Teaching Mixed Methods

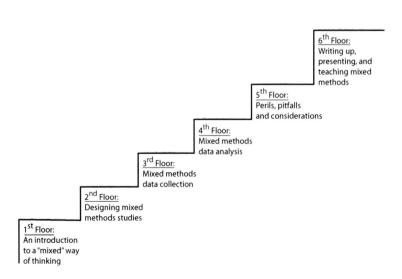

6th Floor:
Writing up, presenting, and teaching mixed methods

5th Floor:
Perils, pitfalls and considerations

4th Floor:
Mixed methods data analysis

3rd Floor:
Mixed methods data collection

2nd Floor:
Designing mixed methods studies

1st Floor:
An introduction to a "mixed" way of thinking

In this final chapter we discuss writing up, presenting, and teaching mixed methods. We also revisit the importance of rigor in mixed methods research, as well as the need to confirm rigor in our mixed methods writing and presentations. This chapter includes a brief description of some peer-reviewed journals and their receptivity to and publication of mixed method studies. We also provide an overview of the types of diagrams used in mixed methods research, as well as helpful hints for communicating results of a mixed methods study to various audiences. Since some readers will likely be teaching mixed methods either as a stand-alone course or in a session on mixed methods in their qualitative or quantitative courses, we describe some teaching models for conveying mixed methods material alone and its placement within existing courses. We begin with how to write up mixed methods, first as a study proposal then as a final, mixed methods report.

WRITING UP MIXED METHODS

This section on writing up mixed methods is divided into two subsections. The first subsection covers writing mixed methods proposals, and the second section describes writing mixed methods reports. As we acknowledge the overlap across writing proposals for theses, dissertations, and funding agencies, we discuss these collectively, providing the reader with specific distinctions where appropriate.

Writing Mixed Methods Proposals

We begin by discussing the structure for writing a mixed methods proposal for federal funding. A useful resource for thinking about how to write a mixed methods proposal for funding is the 2011 handbook *Best Practices for Mixed Methods Research in the Health Sciences* (Creswell, Klassen, Plano Clark, & Clegg Smith, 2011; see http://obssr. od.nih.gov/mixed_methods_research/). This report was commissioned by the Office of Behavioral and Social Sciences Research to experts on mixed methods. Authors for this report include several mixed methods scholars mentioned throughout our pocket guide, such as John W. Creswell, Ann Carroll Klassen, Vicki Plano Clark, and Katherine Clegg Smith. *Best Practices for Mixed Methods Research in the Health Sciences* provides details for what one should include in the specific aims, significance, research strategy, and approach sections of a mixed methods proposal for federal funding. In the following paragraphs, we briefly discuss each of these sections.

Specific aims are the objectives of the proposed research and likely describe quantitative questions or hypotheses, qualitative questions, and/ or mixed methods research questions. Specific aims should also describe the impact the proposed research will have (called the "public health relevance"), the reasons for using mixed methods, and how the study will advance our understanding of the phenomenon of interest. The next section of a mixed methods proposal is called the *research strategy*. This section is usually made up of (a) the significance, (b) the innovation, and (c) the research approach. The significance section is where the researcher provides a backdrop of the topic by synthesizing any current studies and supplemental literature. This review of the literature also helps to frame the importance of the problem and how the proposed project will improve scientific knowledge, technical capability, and/or clinical practice. The significance section of a mixed methods proposal may also include a brief description for how the field will be changed if the proposed aims are achieved and how mixed methods will enhance the study of the problem.

In the innovation section, the researcher discusses how the proposed study challenges current research or clinical practice paradigms. Also included are any novel concepts, methodologies, instrumentation or intervention(s) to be developed or used, and the advantage(s) of using such concepts. The innovation section should also include any refinements, improvements, or new applications of concepts, methodologies, instrumentation, or interventions, as well as any information about the innovative use of mixed methods to address the research problem under study.

The final section of the mixed methods research strategy is the research approach section. This section includes the overall strategy, methodology, and analyses to be used in the project. The approach section is also where the researcher will likely provide some additional information about the use of mixed methods, such as a definition of mixed methods research (complete with references) and a description of the type of mixed methods design that will be implemented in the study. To further illustrate the design, the researcher should also include a diagram of procedures, with clear sections for the data collection and the data analysis plans (which should be organized according to the mixed methods design). To demonstrate the rigor of the research plan, we also recommend including sections on validity (for both quantitative and qualitative phases, then collectively, for the mixed methods study) and potential difficulties and limitations for the study, as well as how these challenges will be addressed, should they arise.

Other information to include in the approach section includes a tentative sequence or timeline of activities for the project and benchmarks for success. This section of the proposal should also include details about the feasibility and the management of any high-risk aspects of the proposed work. Any procedures, situations, or materials that may be hazardous to personnel should be noted and the precautions exercised under such situations described. Finally, the approach section may include preliminary studies (which can include results from a pilot test), as well as the experiences and competency of the researchers who plan to undertake the mixed methods project.

Over the years we have been funded for mixed methods studies because of the uniqueness of our topic areas, as well as the creativity we have demonstrated through our mixing of the methods. Like many scholars, the first few mixed methods proposals that we submitted were not funded due to several competing factors. Thinking back to those early years, we now realize that during that time we were still trying to find our identities in the field, which resulted in mixed methods proposals with clear gaps in utility, relevance, and experience. However, as time and experience has shown us, the more we worked through the kinks from our earlier mixed methods proposals, demonstrated the rigor of our work, and were able to provide evidence for both the utility of our methods and the need for them to examine our areas of interest, we were able to have our mixed methods projects successfully funded. We believe that as interest in and excitement about mixed methods research continue to grow in social work and other health and human service professions, we will continue to witness an increase in the number of agencies (e.g., federal, foundation, local, etc.) whose goals are aligned with what mixed methods projects have to offer.

Writing Mixed Methods Reports: General Tips

At the very early stages of a mixed methods study, an important question researchers should ask themselves is: "How should I write up this mixed methods report?" Perhaps another question to ask is: "What models are there for writing up mixed methods research?" Unfortunately there is a lack of exemplary studies that demonstrate various ways of writing up evidence based on different mixed methods designs; although we are hopeful that this will change in the future due to the current popularity of mixed methods research across multiple disciplines. Even so, different disciplines often have different preferences for how their scholars write up mixed methods research. Also, the lack of models for how to write up mixed methods research is not surprising since, as we know, the process itself is not straightforward. For one thing, academic journals tend to be organized around disciplines and may favor particular types of research conducted within that discipline. Moreover, different types of data analyses may sit awkwardly together on the published page and require a lot of space to justify their validity and credibility within one study. In this section, we discuss writing up mixed methods studies for peer-reviewed journal articles, theses, and doctoral dissertations. But first we offer some general tips for writing up mixed methods.

Whether planning for a mixed methods peer-reviewed journal article, a theses, or a dissertation, we offer the following six tips for writing up a mixed methods research report: (1) start writing as soon as possible, (2) make sure the results are succinct and understandable, (3) ask for feedback from others, (4) recognize that there is a structure to writing everything, (5) match the writing structure to the research design, and (6) learn from examples of mixed methods research in the literature (see Table 6.1). In the subsequent paragraphs, we discuss these six tips in detail.

Our first tip for writing a mixed methods report is to *start writing as soon as possible*. When the time comes to write up mixed methods reports, novice researchers often think that they must start from "scratch." On the contrary, we have found it particularly useful to begin

Table 6.1. Tips for Writing a Mixed Methods Report

1. Start writing as soon as possible.
2. Make sure the results are succinct and understandable.
3. Ask for feedback from others.
4. Recognize that there is a structure to writing everything.
5. Match the writing structure to the research design.
6. Learn from examples in the mixed methods literature.

working on the reports for mixed methods studies as soon as the study begins. That way, materials that have been used to develop the study proposal (and seek funding for the study) can be reused in the final reports. Although we usually think about report writing as the final step in the research process, we have found that a good deal of the work can (and often does) take place before the data are even collected. For example, a background section can often be developed using material from the original mixed methods proposal. While some aspects of the methodology and methods may deviate from the original proposal as the study progresses, most of the background information (e.g., review of the literature, nature of the problem, project goals) remain the same throughout the report. Understandably, text about the mixed methods findings, conclusions, and recommendations generally cannot be written until the study has ended. Most grant proposals (and other proposals that seek financial support for research) require information that builds the case for why the study is important and what kind of impact the study will have on its target group. This is the same kind of information that is needed to craft a final report, so the researcher can copy and paste the information from the proposal into the final report and then edit this information according to the guidelines set in place by the funding agency or the peer-reviewed journal.

Due to the considerable amount of data researchers must collect while conducting a mixed methods study, it is generally a good idea to organize study notes as early as possible but, at the very least, before, during, and after the completion of the study. These notes often serve as a starting point for the mixed methods data collection and management plan that might be included in the final report. Also, preparing written text soon after the start of the data collection activity for both qualitative and quantitative studies helps to classify the concepts, display the data, and reduce the overall volume of data that will eventually need to be analyzed, summarized, and reported at the end of the study. Finally, preparing sections of the final report during the data collection phase (e.g., organizing data by the goals of the study) allows researchers to generate preliminary conclusions or identify potential trends that can be confirmed or refuted with additional data collection activities.

Our second tip for writing mixed methods reports is *ensure the results are succinct and understandable.* A large amount of information is generally collected during a mixed methods study, so it is very easy to become overwhelmed. With so much information at their fingertips, researchers may find themselves asking questions like "What information should I present?" This is oftentimes a very challenging aspect of reporting; however, as a rule of thumb, it is not necessary to report every unit of qualitative and quantitative data collected. In fact, we have found that only a fraction of the qualitative and quantitative data should be discussed and displayed in any mixed methods report. For instance, qualitative field work and data collection methods yield a large volume of text data—apart from the quantitative data—so researchers who try to incorporate all of the qualitative data they have collected into their final report risk losing their audience. In addition, a report that is dominated by a qualitative study may face challenges (e.g., space limitations) with presenting the strengths of the quantitative data and/or the advantages of integrating the two data phases.

On the contrary, omitting too much information from the final mixed methods report risks overlooking the context that helps readers attach meaning to the report's conclusions. One method for limiting the volume of information reported in a mixed methods report is to include only the information that is tied to the original research questions. In other words, regardless of how interesting an anecdote may seem, if it does not relate to one of the original research questions, it probably does not belong in the final report. That is not to say that one could not write a subsequent report that highlights interesting results that surfaced from the data and use the anecdote in *that* report, but usually the initial report that comes out of a mixed methods project focuses primarily on the findings associated with the original purpose and research questions. Once the initial report is completed, all subsequent reports may vary in focus, writing style, and audience.

The information needs of an audience is the deciding factor for how subsequent reports should be developed. Thinking about who is most likely to act on the report's findings may help in the preparation of a useful and illuminating narrative and in the disposal of anecdotes and other data points that are irrelevant to the needs of the readers. When writing mixed methods reports, researchers should ensure that the quantitative findings are tied to the original research question(s), as well as to the qualitative findings of the study. Keep in mind that regardless of how interesting the statistics are, if they are not linked to the original intent of the study, and if a clear description for why and how the mixing occurred is not provided, the quality of the overall study will suffer. This tip also holds true for presentations of mixed methods results, which we discuss later in this chapter.

The third tip for writing up mixed methods results is to *ask for feedback from others*. It is useful to ask colleagues to review sections of the report as their review can help identify omissions and misinterpretations and may elicit new details or insights that were not obvious while initially drafting the final report. An early review of the mixed methods report may also circumvent angry denials after the report becomes public, although there is no guarantee that controversy and demands for changes will not follow the publication of a report. Despite this, however, it is important to keep project staff, respondents, and other stakeholders "in the loop" regarding the data that were collected and how the data were used, all while maintaining and honoring requests for anonymity and/or confidentiality of the study participants. De-identified data (or data with no identifying information of the study participants) is a necessity when writing reports from a mixed methods study. This kind of data can be shared with project staff, study participants, and other stakeholders involved in the research without the risk of participants' identities being revealed. The extent to which other portions of the write-up should be shared with stakeholders depends on the nature of the project and the sample. But generally, it is best to solicit feedback from respondents before the final dissemination of the report to all stakeholders.

The fourth tip for writing up mixed methods research is to *recognize that there is a structure to writing everything*. We mention this here because we often work with students and colleagues who are shocked to see how difficult it is to write a mixed methods report. There is a certain structure to writing mixed methods reports, just like there is a structure to writing book reports, case files, policy briefs, and editorials. The best strategy to use when writing a mixed methods report is to, first and foremost, recognize that the structure of a mixed methods report may be unlike many of the other types of reports one has written before. Therefore we recommend researchers familiarize themselves with various examples of mixed methods reports. These can be found in peer-reviewed journal articles accessed through libraries and scientific article databases. On the other hand, gathering sample mixed methods reports may be as easy as walking the 5 or 10 paces to the offices of mentors and colleagues. Within one's own department, agency, or city, supervisors and/or colleagues may have a library of mixed methods references and evaluation reports that they would be willing to share. Even if they cannot put their hands on the report, they can often refer a researcher to the person who can, or provide contact information for colleagues who can assist with accessing the report.

The fifth tip for writing up mixed methods reports is to *match the writing structure to the research design.* By this we simply mean to structure the writing of the mixed methods report in the same way the study design was structured. For example, if a researchers is using an explanatory sequential design (which involves conducting the quantitative phase first, followed by a qualitative phase), he or she should consider writing the mixed methods report in the same sequence. For this type of design researchers should consider describing the details of their quantitative phase first, then describing the procedures used to build the qualitative component of the study from the quantitative findings. The mixed methods report will likely be much easier for readers to follow if the writing structure is matched to the research design, because in this case it is much easier to use one's thinking pattern to guide their writing pattern. This also helps outsiders see that the researcher is being consistent with his or her use of a certain mixed methods design throughout the study, during implementation, data analyses, and the presentation of the findings. The same holds true if one is conducting an exploratory sequential study in which the qualitative phase is conducted first, followed by the quantitative phase. If researchers are writing up a concurrent design, they should consider guiding the reader through the various stages of the mixed methods procedures and alternating their explanation of each phase, followed by a concise section of the report in which they discuss how the two study phases were integrated for the purposes of achieving the study goals and objectives.

Our final tip for writing up mixed methods reports is to *learn from examples of mixed methods research in the literature.* Reviewing the previous literature on mixed methods research is certainly more than just reading other articles. Researchers should do a very close read of the articles and identify common language, designs, and writing styles. This is an important tip when writing mixed methods reports because, oftentimes, other published mixed methods studies can clue one in to certain jargon that can then be incorporated into the study; it can also provide references that researchers can follow up on when writing the mixed methods report. Citations help grow the field and move a particular area of study forward. Reviewing previously published articles on mixed methods studies also means that researchers will learn more about the designs and procedures in their area of interest and will know how those designs and procedures have been used in prior studies. Also, using citations to other mixed methods articles, books, and successful studies adds credibility to a mixed methods report, as well as the mixed methods study overall.

One of the most rewarding experiences that we have had while reviewing previous mixed methods work by our colleagues is recognizing our colleagues' abilities to clearly explain a new design, method, analysis technique, or innovative way to present mixed methods data. We consider ourselves lifelong learners, so we relish in the opportunity to review creative ways of presenting mixed methods studies by our colleagues and students. Also, at the very least, reviewing other mixed methods reports has taught us how to extend our own thinking and use of mixed methods research. Reviewing the work of others also helps us learn from the mistakes of others. Seeing how others navigate the potential challenges associated with mixed methods research, and being able to anticipate those challenges and have some resources to help address them, can be useful to researchers as they move forward with a mixed methods study. One of the most challenging aspects of any mixed methods study is ascertaining models for reporting mixed methods to a wide array of audiences, and we appreciate reviewing the work of others to see how they have done it.

Writing Up Mixed Methods for Peer-Reviewed Journals

In this section we discuss the structure for writing a mixed methods article for a peer-reviewed journal. For the most part we think journals are becoming more receptive of mixed methods submissions. Overall we believe that journal editors do not necessarily *dislike* mixed methods manuscripts (and thereby reject them outright). Instead, we believe that writing up mixed methods is difficult to do, and that it is even more difficult to do it well and within the submission limitations of a peer-reviewed journal. Despite this, we think that most journal editors would be open (maybe even thrilled?) to consider a mixed methods manuscript for publication in their journal, especially if it is a particularly strong mixed methods manuscript. In the following section we provide some strategies for making sure that a mixed methods manuscript is strong and given full consideration for publication in a peer-reviewed journal.

The structure for a standard mixed methods journal article should start with a strong mixed methods title. We have alluded to this earlier in the chapter and emphasize the importance of this as researchers consider writing up a mixed methods study for publication in a peer-reviewed journal. Many times, the title of a manuscript is the first clue that an editor has as to whether he or she will consider the manuscript for publication (or at least send it out for peer review), so make sure the title is clear, is striking, and can capture the attention of a (potentially overworked) journal editor.

Next the introduction should include a statement of the problem, the issue, a brief literature review of the research problem or issue, any deficiencies in previous studies (e.g., incorporate the need for collecting both quantitative and qualitative data), the audiences for the study, the purpose statement, and research questions. This should be followed by a comprehensive yet concise literature review on the topic area, as well as a review and synthesis of the way the topic has been addressed using other methods. The methods section should include the overall approach and definition of mixed methods research (pending the discipline and journal), the type of mixed methods design used (define, give reasons for using the design, cite studies using the design in the field), a diagram of procedures (which may be included as an appendix), the process for data collection (order data collection according to the design), the plan for data analysis (order data analyses according to the design), and any evidence of rigor that corresponds to both the qualitative and the quantitative phases of the study.

The results section should include a presentation of the data as merged results and be written in a style that is aligned with the selected mixed methods design: convergent, sequential, embedded, transformative, or multiphase. Over the years we have seen some mixed methods journal articles present the findings as separate quantitative and qualitative results, with the data merging in the discussion section of the article. Given this, we believe that the discussion section should include a brief summary of the results (merged or connected) and a statement of future research, study limitations, and a reiteration of the unique contribution of the study to the larger body of knowledge. In Table 6.2 we provide some elements of "good" mixed methods research for peer-reviewed journal articles. We posit that successfully crafting a

Table 6.2. Writing Mixed Methods Reports: Ideas from the Experts

Title	Use the words "mixed methods." Also, create neutral title words that do not lean toward a qualitative or quantitative approach.
Abstract	Include information about the type of mixed methods design used.
Problem statement	Consider the reason for using mixed methods, and hint at this reason as a deficiency in past research.
Write a good mixed methods purpose statement	Include (a) general intent; (b) quantitative and qualitative purpose, data collection, and analysis; (c) a specific reason for mixing and how mixing occurred in the study.
Research questions (if included)	State a quantitative question (or hypotheses), a qualitative question, and a mixed methods question.
Mixed methods design	Identify the type of design used, draw a visual figure, define the design type, and give reasons for including the design (if not redundant with other information).
Quantitative and qualitative methods	Include detailed descriptions of separate quantitative and qualitative methods such as specific forms of quantitative and qualitative designs (e.g., correlational, grounded theory), recruitment procedures, sample selection, sample size, forms of data collection, topics related to data collection (e.g., validity, reliability of scores on instruments), and types of data analysis.
Results	Report quantitative and qualitative results separately or concurrently. Ensure that results are consistent with the flow of the design and the priority given to the quantitative and qualitative sections.
Discussion	Report general quantitative and qualitative results for the study.
Limitations	Identify any challenges that arose during the mixed methods design.
Future research	Talk about how the study adds to the mixed methods literature and opens up further lines for investigation.

Source: Creswell (2015).

mixed methods peer-reviewed journal article is more of an art than a science. As such, some of our colleagues have published recommendations on writing and publishing mixed methods studies (Creswell, 2015; Curry & Nunez-Smith, 2015).

When writing a mixed methods peer-reviewed journal article, researchers should always keep the audience in mind. As is evident by now, much of what it takes to write mixed methods reports is similar across various writing outlets. Thus the focus of researchers' efforts may not always be on *what* they write but rather *how* they write it. Remember while writing, however, that the audience may not be familiar with mixed methods studies and/or how they are completed. For every section of the report, researchers should ask: "What kind of information do I need to provide to my audience to help them interpret my results?" In the next section, we discuss decisions that need to be made when disseminating mixed methods research in peer-reviewed journals.

Decisions Around Disseminating Mixed Methods Research in Peer-Reviewed Journals

When making decisions about how to disseminate mixed methods research through the used of a peer-reviewed journal article, there are a few important considerations. Here we underscore three that are particularly relevant to social workers: the researcher's familiarity with the types of journals that publish mixed methods research, the timing for dissemination, and matters regarding career advancement based on the amount and quality of one's scholarship. We discuss each of these in the subsequent paragraphs.

Familiarity with peer-reviewed journals. Social work researchers may already be familiar with peer-reviewed social work journals in which to publish their work. Some of these journals include *Research on Social Work Practice, Social Work, Social Work and Health, Social Work and Mental Health, Social Services Review,* and *Qualitative Social Work.* This is certainly not an exhaustive list of all the journals that would be open to reviewing a mixed methods submission, and (depending on the topic of the mixed methods study) we encourage researchers to also consider submitting their manuscripts to journals from other disciplines. Since readers with a background in social work are more likely to know about the social work journals listed here, we provide a short list of methods-focused journals below that are mixed methods "friendly" and would welcome the opportunity to consider a mixed methods article. This also is not an exhaustive list; however, it could serve as a starting point for readers' mixed methods research outlets and may be off the current publication radar. These and other journals may also be interested in high-quality mixed methods papers.

One journal that is especially mixed methods friendly is the *Journal of Mixed Methods Research*. It was launched in 2007 and is an innovative, quarterly, interdisciplinary, international publication that focuses on empirical, methodological, and theoretical articles about mixed methods research across the social, behavioral, health, and human sciences. The journal's scope includes delineating where mixed methods research may be used most effectively, illuminating design and procedure issues, and determining the logistics of conducting mixed methods research (http://mmr.sagepub.com/).

We also encourage readers to consider submitting work to the *International Journal of Social Research Methodology*. An important feature of this journal is the mix of academic and theoretically focused methodological articles, articles relating to research and practice in professional and service settings, and those considering the relationship between the two. Given social work's position in research and practice in various settings, we believe that this may be a fantastic outlet for mixed methods research conducted by social workers. The journal addresses an audience of researchers within academic and other research organizations, as well as practitioner-researchers in the field, and provides (a) a focus for ongoing and emerging methodological debates across a range of approaches, both qualitative and quantitative and mixed and comparative methods, as these relate to philosophical, theoretical, ethical, political, and practical issues; (b) an international medium for the publication of discussions of social research methodology and practices across a wide range of social science disciplines and substantive interests; and (c) a forum for researchers based in all sectors to consider and evaluate methods as these relate to research practice (http://www.tandfonline.com/toc/tsrm20/current#.VKSyY_ldX6c).

Given the European angle of the *International Journal of Quantitative and Qualitative Research Methods (IJQQRM)*, it may be a lesser known journal for social workers looking to publish their mixed methods studies in an international outlet. The *IJQQRM* is run by the European Centre for Research, Training and Development (United Kingdom) and publishes academic, theoretical, and methodological articles relating to quantitative, qualitative, and research in professional and service settings. The *IJQQRM* publishes on issues addressed by researchers within academic and independent research organizations and focuses on the ongoing and emerging methodological debates across methods, including mixed and comparative methods relating to philosophical, theoretical, ethical, political, and practical issues. The *IJQQRM* is also an international medium for the publication of social research methodology and practices across a wide range of disciplines and an avenue for researchers in different sectors to consider and evaluate methods as these relate to research practice (http://www.eajournals.org/journals/international-journal-of-quantitative-and-qualitative-research-methods-ijqqrm/).

Timing for dissemination. The proposed timeline for disseminating a mixed methods report can be determined by several different factors, such as the actual results themselves and the recommendations of the stakeholders. Timing the dissemination of the mixed methods results based on the results themselves means the researchers determine which aspects of the data will be shared with the stakeholders and the general public at which points in time. For example, if one aspect of the mixed methods study (let's say the quantitative phase) is particularly timely given an aspect of social justice that has recently gained some media attention, researchers may decide to write up the quantitative phase of the study first and send this report to a peer-reviewed journal or other publication outlet so that the findings can be assessed in the context of current world events. Timing the dissemination of the findings based on the recommendation of the stakeholders also has several implications. For example, if a mixed methods study about a psychotherapy program generated favorable qualitative findings but unfavorable quantitative findings, researchers may decide to share the findings at the same time and highlight the fact that, despite the statistical results, some aspects of the program in question were particularly favorable in the eyes of the mixed methods study participants.

Career advancement. Another matter influencing how researchers will disseminate their mixed methods research in peer-reviewed journal articles is related to professional development and career advancement. For example, social work faculty members at colleges and universities who must "publish or perish" (so to speak) may decide that it behooves them to separate different pieces of their mixed methods studies and send them to different journals. In the increasingly competitive academic world, certainly, quantity is beginning to be just as important as quality. Therefore if a tenure-track assistant professor can publish two peer-reviewed papers instead of one, he or she may jump at the opportunity, as publishing two articles in high-impact journals may put him or her in a much more favorable position for tenure and promotion.

Researchers interested in disseminating their mixed methods research across several different publication outlets can do this in at least three different ways: (a) by separating the qualitative phase from the project and publishing those results separately, (b) by separating the quantitative phase from the rest of the project and publishing those results separately, and (c) by publishing the results from both the qualitative and the quantitative study phases together (see Figure 6.1).

Researchers who decide to publish quantitative and qualitative papers from their mixed methods study in separate peer-reviewed journals should make sure they have clear references and links to the other article(s) in the series of papers. Also, they should reach out to the editors of these journals to see if they would allow them to publish concurrent or sequential quantitative and qualitative papers in the same journal. Researchers may also find it useful to try to publish a single article that describes and integrates both methods and findings

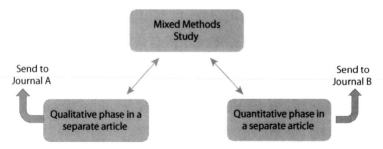

Figure 6.1. Strategy for publishing mixed methods research.

and draws overarching lessons (with or without details in appendices) in one journal. That way, they can have at least one complete mixed methods article in the peer-reviewed literature to which they can reference all of their subsequent articles. Another way to ensure readers have enough information about a mixed methods study to interpret the findings is to offer Internet-based resources that serve as a gateway to one's mixed methods study procedures, protocols, and methodological underpinning. In the technology-savvy era in which we currently live, it can take just a few minutes to develop an online discussion for readers and invited commentators to foster cross-disciplinary communities of knowledge.

Writing Up Mixed Methods for Theses and Dissertations

A mixed methods dissertation or thesis should first and foremost have a title that alerts readers to the fact that it is a mixed methods study. As we have mentioned earlier in this text, it should have an introduction that is comprised of a clear research problem, previous literature on the problem, weaknesses in the previous research, and why the issue warrants using qualitative and quantitative data. The introduction should include a few sentences that allude to why audiences will benefit from reading the thesis or dissertation, followed by a clear purpose statement that addresses the purposes of the project and the reason for the mixed methods design. Research questions that are arranged in a way that matches the design of the study should come after the purpose statement, followed by a discussion of the philosophical and theoretical foundations of the thesis or dissertation that includes sufficient details about the researcher's worldview and the theoretical lens through which he or she wants the reader to read the work (Mertens, 2010). The literature review may include previous studies that have used qualitative, quantitative, or mixed methods to address a similar problem. The methods section of course includes details about the mixed methods design along with any citations from mixed methods references. Table 6.3 summarizes these sections.

Theses or dissertation committee members will want to confirm that a researcher has adhered to the ethical protection of human subjects during his or her research, so any potential ethical issues, resources and skills, a timeline for completing the study, references, and an appendix,

Table 6.3. Important Features to Include in a Mixed Methods Theses or Dissertation

- Definition of mixed methods research
- The type of design used and its definition
- Challenges in using this design; how they are addressed
- Examples of use of the type of design
- Reference to and inclusion of a procedural diagram
- Quantitative data collection and analysis
- Qualitative data collection and analysis and qualitative data transformation, if used (in exploratory design, place qualitative before quantitative)
- Mixed methods data analysis procedures
- Validity approaches

complete with instruments, protocols, and procedural diagrams, should be provided. There are several different ways of structuring a mixed methods thesis or dissertation, especially now, as more doctoral committees are allowing students to choose between a traditional, five-chapter dissertation and the more contemporary, three-article dissertation (which includes an introduction, three self-contained articles written in the style of a peer-reviewed publication, and a conclusion). Given the variation of mixed methods theses and dissertations, we refer readers to other resources after which they can model their work (Ivankova, 2002). In Figure 6.2 we provide a sample structure for students who are interested in using mixed methods to answer the research questions posed in their thesis or dissertation research.

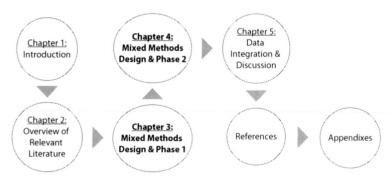

Figure 6.2. Sample structure for a mixed methods thesis or dissertation.

PRESENTING MIXED METHODS RESEARCH

We could argue that presenting the findings from a mixed methods study is the most important step in the research process, because this is when researchers have an opportunity to share not only what they found during the research process itself but also what they found while using qualitative and quantitative approaches to answer the research questions. Researchers should consider several factors when presenting mixed methods research in a professional setting. The subsequent paragraphs on presenting mixed methods research are organized into two types of presentations: visual and oral.

Visual Presentations

One of the most amazing (and underappreciated) talents is the ability to translate complex data concepts (i.e., text) into a visually appealing representation of research. Unfortunately, sometimes mixed methods scholars loathe the idea of "drawing" a diagram to represent a study. However, we find it one of the most fulfilling parts of the mixed methods research process. We do not like pictures because they are "pretty" but rather because they can translate even the most complex concepts into a form of communication that readers can understand. Even if a researcher does not consider himself (or herself) a "picture person," the value of a clear and concise image is undeniable. If developed with careful thought and attention paid to the multiple interpretations of one visual diagram, a picture can truly be worth a thousand words.

So why are visual representations important in mixed methods? First, mixed methods designs are sometimes complex, and mixed methods reports tend to be lengthy, due to the combination of both qualitative and quantitative study phases. Therefore a visual representation of the mixed methods design can not only save space in a report or manuscript, but it can also serve as supplemental information that attracts various types of readers. There are several types of visual presentations in mixed methods research, and each of them can represent different phases of the mixed methods research process. Some of them are similar in nature and structure but are called by different names. In the next section, we discuss the three most common visual presentations used in mixed methods research: design diagrams, procedural diagrams, and joint data displays.

Design Diagram

A design diagram is used to frame the mixed methods design for a mixed methods study. These diagrams have already been explained and alluded to several times thus far throughout this pocket guide. Examples of these diagrams are the exploratory sequential design, the explanatory sequential design, and the convergent design. Design diagrams are usually one of the first aspects of a mixed methods study that a research team develops and agrees on. This type of diagram is usually included in proposals to fund mixed methods research, as well as reports that disseminate final study results. Design diagrams are usually simple and "clean." They offer a minimal description for how the qualitative and quantitative data will be treated in the mixed methods study. They are not crowded with details but rather reduce the complexity of mixed methods by offering a simple and easy way to describe the "flow" of the study. Boxes (solid line and dotted line), circles, and directional arrows are used in design diagrams, just as they are with the six mixed methods designs that we have presented throughout this pocket guide. Design diagrams are especially helpful for the mixed methods novice, or those who are most comfortable with a single-method study and may require a little convincing of the usefulness and value of a mixed methods design.

Procedural Diagram

A procedural diagram is an extension of the design diagram in that it offers a little more detail than the simple design diagram. For us, the procedural diagram is usually the second version of our design diagram in that it provides more detail about the sample type and size, data analysis techniques, and data integration and interpretation (Creswell, 2015). In terms of space, the procedural diagram is a little more crowded than the design diagram but not as crowded as the joint display. Similar to design diagrams, procedural diagrams also include boxes, circles, and directional arrows; the only difference is that each of these may include more details about each particular step (or technique) used in the mixed methods process. Ivankova and colleagues (2006, 2007, 2010) provide useful guidelines for developing procedural diagrams. These guidelines are presented in Table 6.4.

Table 6.4. Guidelines for Drawing Procedural Diagrams

1. Title the diagram.
2. Choose a horizontal or a vertical layout.
3. Draw boxes for the quantitative and qualitative data collection, analysis, and interpretation.
4. Include mixed methods research notation (e.g., uppercase and lowercase letters to designate priority).
5. Use arrows to show the flow of procedures.
6. Specify procedures.
7. Specify expected products or outcomes.
8. Use concise language.

Source: Ivankova et al. (2006).

Joint Data Display

A joint data display is a design used to demonstrate how the qualitative and quantitative data are integrated. There are various ways to develop a joint data display; however, an integral part of any joint data display is the linkages that researchers make between the qualitative and quantitative data. Usually the visual benefits of a joint data display are most appreciated when designs are particularly complicated and for projects that involve several interwoven stages. The joint data display has been examined by mixed methods scholars for years and may be called by different names (Curry & Nunez-Smith, 2015; Fetters et al., 2013). Nevertheless, it is clear that a visual representation of the ways in which qualitative and quantitative data "dance" with one another is of value to social workers engaged in mixed methods studies. We provide a sample joint data display from one of our projects in Figure 6.3.

In his mixed methods primer, Creswell (2015) offers some helpful hints for developing diagrams for a mixed methods study. We agree that whether a researcher is developing a design diagram, a procedural diagram, or a joint data display, the diagram should always have a title, boxes and/or circles to show the data collection and analysis for both quantitative and qualitative research. Diagrams should also include the ordering of the qualitative and quantitative research sequence (with arrows), and it should be no more than one page in length. Creswell suggests starting with a basic mixed methods design and building on the diagram from there.

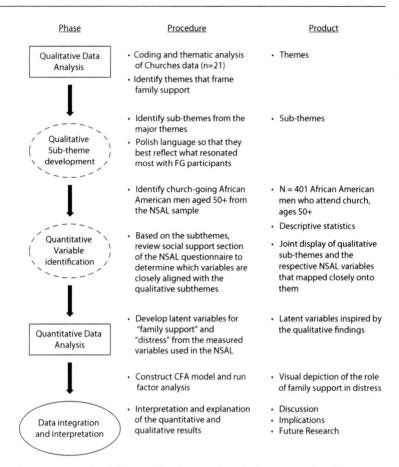

Figure 6.3. Procedural diagram for the mixed methods sequential exploratory design procedures.

Oral Presentations

We could argue that once the visual presentation of a mixed methods study is completed, talking about the study becomes a fairly simple (and enjoyable) pastime. Certainly a researcher can visualize his or her diagram if caught in an elevator with a colleague who asks about some of his or her more recent projects. Likewise, if researchers need to share information about their mixed methods study with a stakeholder, the latter would be thrilled to receive a one-page diagram of the project rather than a 25-page report with no visual presentations. To avoid redundancy, we do not cover the same information presented in the visual representation section here. Rather we discuss our recommendations for presenting mixed methods research in some of the more common oral presentation settings. Our list is not exhaustive; however, the recommendations we provide here can be transferable to other oral presentation settings. In the following section we provide recommendations for presenting a mixed methods research at a conference, in a guest lecture (classroom) setting, during a quick conversation with colleagues, and to clients.

Conference Presentation

If a researcher is invited to present his or her mixed methods research at a conference or professional meeting, it is safe to assume that representatives of the group are not only interested in the study topic but also the methodological decisions behind how the researcher came to his or her study results and conclusions. If presenting at a disciplinary conference (e.g., psychology, anthropology, sociology) or one sponsored by a particular profession (i.e., social work and public health), researchers will probably need to (metaphorically) "walk" the audience through the research question, the need for further exploration of such a question, the methodological decisions made during the research study, and how the qualitative and quantitative results were integrated to answer the research question(s). They should also describe their mixed methods team and the strengths (and weaknesses) of each member.

Unless researchers are presenting their mixed methods study at the Mixed Methods International Research Association Conference, they may meet some naysayers about mixed methods research and its utility. Of course it is not in a researcher's best interest to argue with audience naysayers or rattle off the reasons why he or she is the most qualified person to conduct a mixed methods study. Much more important is the articulation of the rigor that the researcher ensured at every step of the process and how mixing the methods, data, and results were truly an advantage to the project goals and objectives. We also advise that if researchers find themselves in a bit of a verbal "scuffle" with one or more audience members, they should kindly nod, smile, and then offer to have a conversation with that person(s) after the presentation has ended.

Classroom Setting (Guest Lecture)

For academicians in particular, the classroom setting is most likely the first real opportunity that a researcher will have to present a mixed methods study. It is a good idea to treat the classroom presentation as a "dry run" for one's mixed methods study presentation. Over the years we have found students to be very gracious audiences, as they are often perplexed about many of the same issues as the experts in the field. We have also found that if researchers inform the students that this is the first time they have presented their mixed methods findings in a public setting, the classroom setting becomes a warm and "even playing field" to discuss the work. Researchers should also encourage students to ask questions and offer suggestions for how to presentation certain aspects of the mixed methods study in the future.

Talking with Colleagues

Any researcher who has ever tried to explain something to his or her colleagues that is outside the scope of the department (or the field) has probably already received "the look." As social work researchers who have "marched to the beat of their own drums" for quite some time now, we are very accustomed to receiving this look from our colleagues. "The look" is that expression that a researcher receives from colleagues when they ask what he or she has been working on lately and the answer is "a mixed methods project" (or any project that may be unfamiliar to colleagues). Usually "the look" conveys uncertainty, confusion, surprise, or sheer annoyance with the fact that the researcher is attempting something off the traditional paths of social work research and practice.

In anticipation of "the look," we advise mixed methods researchers to always have a set of predetermined phrases prepared to help explain to colleagues why such a mixed methods project may be necessary in order for the researcher (not to mention others who are engaged in similar work) to achieve his or her social work research and practice goals. For example, for colleagues who insist that spending too much time doing social work research detracts from time that could be spent with clients, we suggest reminding them that the social work code of ethics calls for "research and evaluation that is rigorous and meaningful," which justifies extending the work of previous social work scholars by conducting social work research that includes a mixed methods design. Remind colleagues who seem concerned about the resources that are required to conduct a mixed methods project that most agencies that receive funding are accustomed to budgeting for the money that is spent. What better way to spend the money than by maximizing the experiences with the clients and collecting different types (i.e., qualitative and quantitative) data that can be used to improve the programs offered by an agency? Lastly, when colleagues question the need for such a large (or diverse, or advanced, etc.) team of individuals to conduct mixed methods research, just smile and inform them that the beauty of the social work profession is that we are able to interact with other professions who also have specialized training and experiences. Social work researchers who strive to evoke change among marginalized communities will do so by collaborating with individuals and teams (across agencies or across disciplines) who are truly the best at what they do.

Talking with Clients

Much like presenting to students, explaining mixed methods projects to clients can be exciting and insightful. Over the years we have found that once we explain the utility of both qualitative and quantitative data in helping us to acquire the "complete picture" of our patients and clients, they are typically on board with whatever aspects of the project they may have been concerned about in the first place. Certainly one is less likely to explain the ins and outs of the mixed methods designs and analysis techniques (i.e., constant comparative analysis and analysis of variance) to clients. However, in appropriate settings, such as during the study recruitment process and/or during the informed consent process, researchers may find it necessary to explain to clients the type of project they are undertaking, the types of data they hope to gather, and why they have determined that a "mixed" way of thinking is the most effective way to obtain the answers to particular social work problems and questions.

TEACHING MIXED METHODS

Along with the growing popularity of mixed methods research is the growing need for teaching mixed methods research skills to aspiring mixed methods enthusiasts. While this is wonderful and exciting for mixed methods as a unique, cross-discipline method, it does put the burden on those of us who do it (and hopefully do it well) to develop resources to help train the next generation of mixed methods researchers. In this section we offer considerations for aspiring teachers of mixed methods research, provide models for teaching mixed methods, and make recommendations for the types of resources to use in mixed methods courses.

Characteristics of "Good" Mixed Methods Teachers in Social Work

Teachers of mixed methods must frame the pedagogic tone for their students on the first day of class. This is important because it serves as a good model for students. If teachers are honest and clear about their pedagogic tone and philosophical stance, then the students can see that there are several ways to adopt and incorporate mixed methods into their own work. In the same vein, we encourage teachers of mixed methods to empower their students to adopt their own pedagogic tone and realize their own philosophical stance (Mertens, 2010). This is a good practice not only when teaching mixed methods in the classroom but also during work with other mixed methods students and trainees. We find that if we do not alert the students to the growing number of dialectic stances, students find themselves prisoners of the one (or two) stances introduced by their mixed methods teachers.

Mixed methods offers scholars the option to adopt certain parts of the methods while at the same time choosing not to adopt others. While presumed chaotic, this is what makes social workers' understanding and adoption of mixed methods so important to their work. Because our clients and research participants do not fit nicely into boxes and tend to have complex lives, mixed methods seems to be most akin to the work that we, as social workers, do every day. Much like social work, mixed methods operates within a loose framework: there are guidelines and "rules" that have been adopted over time, but often (and depending on the circumstance), the guidelines must be modified. A good mixed method teacher should relay this to his or her students.

We also believe that good teachers of mixed methods in social work never lose sight of the importance of context in the work that they do. Mixed methods are pretty popular right now, so graduate students may be tempted to "wow" their thesis or dissertation committees with their mixed methods studies. Similarly, those who may be in social work practice or academia may be tempted to astound their supervisors with evidence-based practice and evidence-based research that uses mixed methods. And of course, social work postdoctoral fellows or faculty members feel the pressure to impress future employers, the department chair, promotion and tenure committees, and funding agencies with their eloquence and expertise with mixed methods. However, we affirm here (just as we have affirmed throughout this pocket guide) that mixed methods should be used only when necessary. We have seen several of our students and colleagues fail at doing mixed methods because they were focused on the methods themselves and not how the social work problem could be resolved using the methods.

Speaking of students, let us not forget that for many mixed methods students, the goal is to *do* mixed methods. Therefore, depending on the length of the course, teachers of mixed methods should be selective about the amount of time spent on the epistemological details surrounding mixed methods (and the time spent discussing such detail). We note this particularly for those teaching mixed methods to social workers who, more often than not, prefer not to be inundated with the theoretical depth of their practice methods. Note that we are not discouraging mixed methods teachers from including important paradigm-specific content in their teaching, but rather we have found success in highlighting the major theoretical underpinnings of mixed methods research, providing students with the resources to further explore these underpinnings on their own, then getting right to the "meat" of social work research that uses mixed methods. Mixed methods, when taught this way, can protect students from becoming distracted by the deep epistemological history of the method and instead help them focus on its importance, provide assistance with framing the methods, then proceed right into the steps necessary to conduct mixed methods research. From our experience, we have found that this approach results in exactly what we want: our students deciding to do a deeper review of the philosophical underpinning on their own and deciding for themselves what their philosophical stances are on these methods, so we can then empower them to raise questions during class about the framing of the decisions we make in a mixed methods study as we proceed through the steps.

Models for Teaching Mixed Methods

Based on our own teaching of mixed methods research over the years, we believe that there are at least two pedagogic models for teaching beginning to advanced mixed methods research to social workers; although we could also consider variations of these teaching models. The first pedagogic model is more for audiences with less formal training and less familiarity with one (or both) of the single-method research methods. This model involves presenting mixed methods research in a sequence, very much like the sequential designs references by our predecessors. So, for the sake of congruency, we call the first pedagogic model the *sequential method teaching model* and the second the *convergent method teaching model.*

The sequential method of teaching model is a three-tiered process that involves (a) teaching quantitative methods, (b) teaching qualitative methods, and then (c) teaching the students how the two are combined to achieve mixed methods. This model allows students to focus on (first) acquiring a deeper understanding for how the single methods function apart from one another, then how to combine them for a successful mixed methods study. Again, this teaching model is particularly successful among students with little to no experience in research methods, data collection, data analysis, and data interpretation and presentation. When using this model, the goal is for students to understand the strengths and weakness of both qualitative and quantitative research individually, as well as how the strengths and weaknesses of both methods are complimented using mixed methods research. Using this pedagogic model, mixed methods teachers present the various research processes to students using the single methods as a framework, then introduce mixed methods framing, designs, analysis, and data integration. With the sequential method teaching model, the goal is not to make students the experts in mixed methods but rather, the goal is to ensure that students are knowledgeable about the ins and outs of the single methods, which in turn, helps them become comfortable with how mixed methods research can be used to answer their research questions.

The convergent method teaching model is a multitiered process that involves guiding the students through the various stages of the research process with mixed methods used as a backdrop. This model is for audiences with more comfort and familiarity using one or both of the single methods and for students who have a desire to learn more about how mixed methods can help them answer their research questions. Because this book is a teaching resource for mixed methods, we hope that the way we have framed it—with a step-by-step process for conducting mixed methods research in nine steps—is a type of convergent method teaching model. With the convergent method teaching model, less attention is given to the single methods alone and more attention is given to how they integrate during each stage of a mixed methods study. While this pedagogic style does spend time underscoring what qualitative and quantitative methods contribute during each step of the research process, its focus is on how each single method converges during each step of the research process to answer the research questions. A major aspect of the convergent method teaching model is teaching the students to determine if mixed methods are necessary, given their problem statement and research questions. Likewise, noting that a rigorous and credible single-method study can be used in place of a mixed methods study is challenged and realized by many of our students when we use this model.

Resources for Teaching Mixed Methods

Before we bring this chapter to a close, we briefly cover how teachers of mixed methods should go about selecting resources for their social work students. When selecting resources for various course and training opportunities, social work instructors usually choose between books and peer-reviewed journal articles. Since social work is such a diverse profession in terms of the types of material that can be taught across the various macro, meso, and micro levels of the profession, depending on the aspect of the profession one hopes to teach, certain teaching resources are preferred. For example, we have found that over the years our colleagues who teach policy tend to lean more toward Internet-based resources and peer-reviewed articles (as opposed to textbooks). This is because the Internet and peer-reviewed journal articles tend to possess the most up-to-date and relevant information on social work policy.

Note that when we say "up-to-date" we realize that scientific journal articles do not usually have the most up-to-date information when compared to the Internet. But for the purposes of teaching policy, we are comparing the use of the Internet and peer-reviewed journal articles to the use of textbooks, which are a more traditional (and oftentimes outdated) teaching resource.

On the other hand, when teaching social work research methods (as we have both done in the past), textbooks tend to be a primary teaching tool. This is because, as far as research methods go, the foundations for social work research methods have not changed. Therefore, when teaching basic social work research methods courses, it makes sense to select a research methods text as the primary reading for the course but to supplement this text with more up-to-date information that provides cutting-edge examples for how research is conducted in real social work settings. There are other resources on teaching mixed methods that are not specific to social work but that we have found helpful in our scholarly endeavors (Bazeley, 2003; Earley, 2007; Mertens, 2010). We encourage readers to review these references and to locate other peer-reviewed articles published in scientific journals of social work and related disciplines, as well as those on the Internet.

SUMMARY

As social workers, our unique contribution to the world is the "lens" through which we see the world, its problems, and the ways in which we take action. Therefore continuing to operationalize the rigor of mixed methods through this lens is a major contribution to our field and our world. We urge readers to give some thought to how their mixed methods studies will be written up and presented long before the writing and presentations begin. Also, we encourage teachers of mixed methods research to consider using as many resources as possible to emphasize to their students the importance of rigor and variation. For example, over the years we have used a combination of books, peer-reviewed journal articles, personal anecdotes, and Internet resources whenever we teach mixed methods. Overall the ways in which mixed methods studies in social work are planned, written up, presented, and taught will guide the advancement of mixed methods in our field and their utility with the individuals and communities we hope to impact.

References

Adelman, H. S., & Taylor, L. (2002). *Student and family assistance programs and services to address barriers to learning: A center training tutorial* (Report No. CG031674). Rockville, MD: Center for Mental Health Services.

Adelman, H. S., & Taylor, L. (2005). *The implementation guide to student learning supports in the classroom and schoolwide: New directions for addressing barriers to learning.* Thousand Oaks, CA: Corwin Press.

Antle, B. J., & Regehr, C. (2003). Beyond individual rights and freedoms: Meta-ethics in social work research. *Social Work, 48*(1), 135–144.

Auerbach, C. F., & Silverstein, L. B. (2003). *Qualitative data: An introduction to coding and analysis.* New York, NY: New York University Press.

Balas, E. A., & Boren, S. A. (2000). Managing clinical knowledge for health care improvement. In J. Bemmel & A. T. McCray (Eds.), *Yearbook of Medical Informatics 2000* (pp. 65–70). Stuttgart: Schattauer.

Banyard, V. L., & Miller, K. E. (1998). The powerful potential of qualitative research for community psychology. *American Journal of Community Psychology, 26*(4), 485–505.

Bazeley, P. (2003). Teaching mixed methods. *Qualitative Research Journal, 3,* 117–126.

Bazeley, P. (2009). Integrating data analyses in mixed methods research. *Journal of Mixed Methods Research, 3*(3), 203–206.

Bernard, H. H. R., & Ryan, G. W. (2009). *Analyzing qualitative data: Systematic approaches.* Thousand Oaks, CA: SAGE.

Bisman, C. (2004). Social work values: The moral core of the profession. *British Journal of Social Work, 34,* 109–123.

Brekke, J. S. (2012). Shaping a science of social work. *Research on Social Work Practice, 22*(5), 455–464.

Bronstein, L. R., & Kovacs, P. J. (2013). Writing a mixed methods report in social work research. *Research on Social Work Practice, 23*(3), 354–360.

Bryman, A. (2006). Integrating quantitative and qualitative research: How is it done? *Qualitative Research, 6*(1), 97–113.

Bryman, A. (2007). Barriers to integrating qualitative and quantitative research. *Journal of Mixed Methods Research, 1*(1), 8–22.

Burke Johnson, R., & Onwuegbuzie, A. J. (2004). Mixed methods research: A research paradigm whose time has come. *Educational Researcher, 33*(7), 14–26.

Burke Johnson, R., Onwuegbuzie, A. J., & Turner, L. A. (2007). Toward a definition of mixed methods research. *Journal of Mixed Methods Research, 1*(2), 112–133.

Cohen, J. (1968). Multiple regression as a general data-analytic system. *Psychological Bulletin, 70,* 426–443.

Cornelius, L. J., & Harrington, D. (2014). *A social justice approach to survey design and analysis.* New York, NY: Oxford University Press.

Crabtree, B. F., & Miller, W. L. (Eds.). (1999). Doing qualitative research (2nd ed.). Thousand Oaks, CA: SAGE.

Creswell, J. W. (2015). *A concise introduction to mixed methods research.* Thousand Oaks, CA: SAGE.

Creswell, J. W., Klassen, A. C., Plano Clark, V. L., & Clegg Smith, K. (2011). *Best practices for mixed methods research in the health sciences.* Washington, DC: Office of Behavioral and Social Sciences Research.

Creswell, J. W., & Plano Clark, V. L. (2011). Designing and conducting mixed methods research (2nd ed.). Thousand Oaks, CA: SAGE.

Creswell, J. W., & Tashakkori, A. (2007). Developing publishable mixed methods manuscripts [Editorial]. *Journal of Mixed Methods Research, 1*(2), 107–111. doi:10.1177/1558689806298644

Cronbach, L. J. (1951). Coefficient alpha and the internal structure of tests. *Psychometrika, 22*(3), 297–334.

Curry, L., & Nunez-Smith, M. (2015). *Mixed methods in health sciences research: A practical primer* (Mixed Methods Research Series 1). Thousand Oaks, CA: SAGE.

Darlington, Y., & Scott, D. (2002). *Qualitative research in practice: Stories from the field.* Buckingham, England: Taylor & Francis.

Dattalo, P. (2008). *Determining sample size: Balancing power, precision, and practicality.* New York, NY: Oxford University Press.

DeWalt, K., & DeWalt, B. (2011). *Participant observation: A guide for fieldworkers*. New York, NY: Rowman & Littlefield.

Drisko, J. (January 2000). *Qualitative data analysis: It's not just anything goes*. Paper presented at the annual meeting of the Society for Social Work and Research, Charleston, SC.

Earley, M. A. (2007). Developing a syllabus for a mixed-methods research course. *International Journal of Social Research Methodology, 10*(2), 145–162.

Elpers, K., & FitzGerald, E. A. (2013). Issues and challenges in gatekeeping: A framework for implementation. *Social Work Education, 32*(3), 286–300.

Epstein, I. (2010). *Clinical data-mining: Integrating practice and research*. New York, NY: Oxford University Press.

Evans, B. C., Coon, D. W., & Ume, E. (2011). Use of theoretical frameworks as a pragmatic guide for mixed methods studies: A methodological necessity? *Journal of Mixed Methods Research, 5*(4), 276–292.

Farquhar, S. A., Parker, E. A., Schulz, A. J., & Israel, B. A. (2006). Application of qualitative methods in program planning for health promotion interventions. *Health Promotion Practice, 7*(2), 234–242.

Fernald, D. H., & Duclos, C. W. (2005). Enhance your team-based qualitative research. *Annals of Family Medicine, 3*(4), 360–364.

Fetters, M. D., Curry, L. A., & Creswell, J. W. (2013). Achieving integration in mixed methods designs—Principles and practices. *Health Services Research, 48*(6), 2134–2156.

Floersch, J. (2000). Reading the case record: The oral and written narratives of social workers. *The Social Service Review, 74*(2), 169–192.

Glaser, B. G., & Strauss, A. L. (1967). *The discovery of grounded theory: Strategies for qualitative research*. Chicago, IL: Aldine.

Greene, J. (2002). Mixed-method evaluation: A way of democratically engaging with difference. *Evaluation Journal of Australasia, 2*(2), 23–29.

Greene, J. C. (2007). *Mixed methods in social inquiry*. San Francisco, CA: Wiley.

Greene, J. C., & Haidt, J. (2002). How (and where) does moral judgment work? *Trends in Cognitive Sciences, 6*(12), 517–523.

Grinnell, R. M., Jr., & Unrau, Y. A. (2014). *Social work research and evaluation: Foundations of evidence-based practice* (10th ed.). New York, NY: Oxford University Press.

Guest, G., & MacQueen, K. (2008). Reevaluating guidelines for qualitative research. In G. Guest & K. MacQueen (Eds.), *Handbook for team-based qualitative research* (pp. 205–226). Lanham, MD: AltaMira.

Haight, W., Kayama, M., Kincaid, T., Evans, K., & Kim, N. K. (2013). The elementary-school function of children with maltreatment histories and mild cognitive or behavioral disturbances: A mixed methods inquiry. *Children and Youth Services Review, 35*(3), 420–428.

Hesse-Biber, S. N. (2010). *Mixed methods research: Merging theory with practice.* New York, NY: Guilford.

Ivankova, N. V. (2002). A sample mixed methods dissertation proposal. Retrieved from http://www.sagepub.com/creswellstudy/Sample%20Student%20Proposals/Proposal-MM-Ivankova.pdf

Ivankova, N. V., Creswell, J. W., & Stick, S. (2006). Using mixed methods sequential explanatory design: From theory to practice. *Field Methods, 18*(1), 3–20.

Ivankova, N. V., & Kawamura, Y. (2010). Emerging trends in the utilization of integrated designs in the social, behavioral, and health sciences. In A. Tashakkori & C. Teddlie (Eds.), *SAGE handbook of mixed methods in social & behavioral research* (2nd ed., pp. 581–611). Thousand Oaks, CA: SAGE.

Ivankova, N., & Stick, S. (2007). Students' persistence in a distributed doctoral program in educational leadership in higher education: A mixed methods study. *Research in Higher Education, 48*(1), 93–135. doi:10.1007/s11162-006-9025-4

Johnson, R. B., Onwuegbuzie, A. J., & Turner, L. A. (2007). Toward a definition of mixed methods research. *Journal of Mixed Methods Research, 1*(2), 112–133.

Kartalova-O'Doherty, Y., & Doherty, D. T. (2009). Satisfied careers of persons with enduring mental illness: Who and why? *International Journal of Social Psychiatry, 55*(3), 257–271.

Kline, R. (2004). *Beyond statistical significance testing: Reforming data analysis methods in behavioral research.* Washington, DC: American Psychological Association.

Krueger, R. A., & Casey, M. A. (2009). *Focus groups: A practical guide for applied research* (4th ed.). Thousand Oaks, CA: SAGE.

Krysik, J., & Finn, J. (2013). *Research for effective social work practice* (3rd ed.). New York, NY: Routledge.

La Pelle, N. (2004). Simplifying qualitative data analysis using general purpose software tools. *Field Methods, 16*(1), 85–108.

Landau, R. (2008). Social work research ethics: Dual roles and boundary issues. *Families in Society, 89*(4), 571–577.

Leech, N. L., & Onwuegbuzie, A. J. (2007). An array of qualitative data analysis tools: A call for data analysis triangulation. *School Psychology Quarterly, 22*, 557–584.

Li, T., Hutfless, S., Scharfstein, D. O., Daniels, M. J., Hogan, J. W. Little, R. J. . . . Dickersin, K. (2014). Standards should be applied in the prevention and handling of missing data for patient-centered outcomes research: A systematic review and expert consensus. *Journal of Clinical Epidemiology, 67*(1),15–32.

Liu, X. (2009). Ordinal regression analysis: Fitting the proportional odds model using Stata, SAS and SPSS. *Journal of Modern Applied Statistical Methods, 8*(2), 632–645.

Lin, W., & Van Ryzin, G. G. (2012). Web and mail surveys: An experimental comparison of methods for nonprofit research. *Nonprofit and Voluntary Sector Quarterly, 41*(6), 1014–1028.

Lincoln, Y., & Guba, E. (1985). *Naturalistic inquiry.* Newbury Park, CA: SAGE.

Longhofer, J., & Floersch, J. (2012). The coming crisis in social work: Some thoughts on social work and science. *Research on Social Work Practice, 22*(5), 499–519.

Longhofer, J., Floersch, J., & Hoy, J. (2012). *Qualitative methods for practice research.* New York, NY: Oxford University Press.

Malai, R. (2012). Social workers face new challenges. *NASW News, 57*(2). Retrieved from http://www.naswdc.org/pubs/news/.

Maxwell, J. A., & Loomis, D. (2003). Mixed methods design: An alternative approach. In A. Tashakkori & C. Teddlie (Eds.), *Handbook of mixed methods in social & behavioral research* (pp. 241–271). Thousand Oaks, CA: SAGE.

Mayoh, J., & Onwuegbuzie, A. J. (2013). Toward a conceptualization of mixed methods phenomenological research. *Journal of Mixed Methods Research.* Advance online publication. doi:10.1177/1558689813505358.

Melnyk, B. M., Morrison-Beedy, D., & Moore, S. M. (2012). Nuts and bolts of designing intervention studies. In B. M. Melnyk & D. Morrison-Beedy (Eds.), *Intervention research: Designing, conducting, analyzing, and funding: A practical guide for success* (pp. 37–64). New York, NY: Springer.

Melnyk, B. M., & Morrison-Beedy, D. (Eds) (2012). *Intervention research: Designing, conducting, analyzing, and funding.* New York, NY: Springer Publishers.

Menon, G. M., & Cowger, C. D. (2010). Integrating qualitative and quantitative research methods. In B. Thyer (Ed.), *The handbook of social work research methods* (2nd ed., pp. 609–613). Thousand Oaks, CA: SAGE.

Mertens, D. M. (2009). *Transformative research and evaluation.* New York, NY: Guilford.

Mertens, D. M. (2010). Philosophy in teaching mixed methods: The transformative paradigm as illustration. *International Journal of Multiple Research Approaches, 4*(1), 9–18.

Mertens, D. M. (2013). Emerging advances in mixed methods: Addressing social justice. *Journal of Mixed Methods Research, 7*(3), 215–218.

Mertens, D. M. (2014). A momentous development in mixed methods research. *Journal of Mixed Methods Research, 8*(1), 3–5.

Miles, M. B., & Huberman, A. M. (1994). *Qualitative data analysis: An expanded sourcebook* (2nd ed.). Thousand Oaks, CA: SAGE.

Miles, M. B., Huberman, A. M., & Saldana, J. (2013). *Qualitative data analysis: A methods sourcebook*. Thousand Oaks, CA: SAGE.

Morgan, D. L., & Krueger, R. A. (Eds.). (1998). *The focus group kit*. Thousand Oaks, CA: SAGE.

Morse, J. M. (1991). Approaches to qualitative-quantitative methodological triangulation. *Nursing Research, 40*(2), 120–123.

Morse, J., & Richards, L. (2002). *Read me first for a user's guide to qualitative research*. Thousand Oaks, CA: SAGE.

Moxley, D., Bishop, J., & Miller-Cribbs, J. (2015). *Photovoice methods in social work: Using visual and narrative techniques in participatory research and practice*. New York, NY: Springer.

National Association of Social Workers. (2014). Code of ethics. Retrieved from https://www.socialworkers.org/pubs/code/code.asp

Nastasi, B. K., Hitchcock, J. H., & Brown, L. M. (2010). An inclusive framework for conceptualizing mixed methods design typologies: Moving toward fully integrated synergistic research models. In A. Tashakkori & C. Teddlie (Eds.), *SAGE handbook of mixed methods in social & behavioral research* (2nd ed., pp. 305–338). Thousand Oaks, CA: SAGE.

Niglas, K. (2007). Media review: Microsoft Office Excel spreadsheet software. *Journal of Mixed Methods Research, 1*(3), 297–299.

O'Cathain, A. (2010). Assessing the quality of mixed methods research: Toward a comprehensive framework. In A. Tashakkori & C. Teddlie (Eds.), *SAGE handbook of mixed methods in social & behavioral research* (2nd ed., pp. 531–558). Thousand Oaks, CA: SAGE.

Oktay, J. S. (2012). *Grounded theory*. New York, NY: Oxford University Press.

Onwuegbuzie, A. J., & Combs, J. P. (2010). Emergent data analysis techniques in mixed methods research. In A. Tashakkori & C. Teddlie (Eds.), *SAGE handbook of mixed methods in social & behavioral research* (2nd ed., pp. 397–430). Thousand Oaks, CA: SAGE.

Orme, J. G., & Combs-Orme, T. (2009). *Multiple regression with discrete dependent variables*. New York, NY: Oxford University Press.

Padgett, D. K. (2008). *Qualitative methods in social work research* (Vol. 36). Thousand Oaks, CA: SAGE.

Padgett, D. K. (2009). Qualitative and mixed methods in social work knowledge development. *Social Work, 54*(2), 101–105.

Peled, E., & Leichtentritt, R. (2002). The ethics of qualitative social work research. *Qualitative Social Work, 1*(2), 145–169.

Rainie, L. (2013). Cell phone ownership hits 91% of adults. Pew Research Center. http://www.pewresearch.org/fact-tank/2013/06/06/cell-phone-ownership-hits-91-of-adults/. Accessed November 5, 2014.

Randolph, K. A., & Myers, L. L. (2013). *Basic statistics: Multivariate analysis.* New York, NY: Oxford University Press.

Reamer, F. (2013). Ethics in qualitative research. In A. E. Fortune, W. J. Reid, & R. L. Miller (Eds.), *Qualitative research in social work* (pp. 35–60). New York, NY: Columbia University Press.

Rosenthal, J. A. (2012). *Statistics and data interpretation for social work.* New York, NY: Springer.

Rubin, A., & Babbie, E. (2013). *Brooks/Cole empowerment series: Research methods for social work* (8th ed.). Belmont, CA: Cengage Learning.

Russell, A. C. (2014). *A hands-on manual for social work research: How to stop worrying and start loving research.* Chicago, IL: Lyceum Books.

Saldaña, J. (2012). *The coding manual for qualitative researchers* (No. 14). Thousand Oaks, CA: SAGE.

Sandelowski, M. (2000). Combining qualitative and quantitative sampling, data collection, and analysis techniques in mixed-methods studies. *Research in Nursing & Health, 23*(3), 246–255.

Sandelowski, M. (2001). Real qualitative researchers do not count: The use of numbers in qualitative research. *Research in Nursing & Health, 24*(3), 230–240.

Sandelowski, M. (2014). Unmixing mixed-methods research. *Research in Nursing & Health, 37*(1), 3–8.

Scourfield, J., & Maxwell, N. (2010). Social work doctoral students in the UK: A web-based survey and search of the index to theses. *British Journal of Social Work, 40*(2), 548–566.

Silverman, D. (2011). *Interpreting qualitative data.* Thousand Oaks, CA: SAGE.

Slife, B. D., & Williams, R. N. (1995). *What's behind the research? Discovering hidden assumptions in the behavioral sciences.* Thousand Oaks, CA: SAGE.

Small, M. L. (2011). How to conduct a mixed methods study: Recent trends in a rapidly growing literature. *Annual Review of Sociology, 37*(1), 57–86.

StataCorp. 2013. *Stata statistical software: Release 13.* College Station, TX: Author.

Stewart, M., Makwarimba, E., Barnfather, A., Letourneau, N., & Neufeld, A. (2008). Researching reducing health disparities: Mixed-methods approaches. *Social Science & Medicine, 66*(6), 1406–1417.

Stockdale, M. S. (2002). Analyzing focus group data with spreadsheets. *American Journal of Health Studies, 18*(1), 55–60.

Swallow, V., Newton, J., & Lottum, C. V. (2003). How to manage and display qualitative data using Framework and Microsoft® Excel. *Journal of Clinical Nursing, 12*, 610–612.

Tashakkori, A., & Creswell, J. W. (2007a). Exploring the nature of research questions in mixed methods research [Editorial]. *Journal of Mixed Methods Research, 1*(3), 207–211.

Tashakkori, A., & Creswell, J. W. (2007b). The new era of mixed methods [Editorial]. *Journal of Mixed Methods Research, 1*(1), 3–7.

Tashakkori, A., & Teddlie, C. (Eds.). (2010). *SAGE handbook of mixed methods in social & behavioral research* (2nd ed., pp. 581–611). Thousand Oaks, CA: SAGE.

Taylor-Powell, E. & Renner, M. (2003). Analyzing qualitative data. University of Wisconsin-Extension. http://learningstore.uwex.edu/assets/pdfs/G3658-12.PDF

Teasley, M., Canfield, J. P., Archuleta, A. J., Crutchfield, J., & McCullough Chavis, A. (2012). Perceived barriers and facilitators to school social work practice: A mixed methods study. *Children & Schools, 34*(3), 145–153.

Thompson, B. (2001). Significance, effect sizes, stepwise methods, and other issues: Strong arguments more the field. *Journal of Experimental Education, 70*, 80–93.

Thompson, B. (2002). What future quantitative social science research could look like: Confidence intervals for effect sizes. *Education Researcher, 31*(3), 24–31.

Thyer, B. A. (2001). What is the role of theory in research on social work practice? *Journal of Social Work Education, 37*(1), 9–25.

Thyer, B. A. (2009). *The handbook of social work research methods.* Thousand Oaks, CA: SAGE.

Thyer, B. A. (2011). LCSW examination pass rates: Implications for social work education. *Clinical Social Work Journal, 39*(3), 296–300.

Ulin, P. R., Robinson, E. T., & Tolley, E. E. (2005). *Qualitative methods in public health: A field guide for applied research.* San Francisco, CA: Jossey-Bass.

Vacha-Haase, T., & Thompson, B. (2004). How to estimate and interpret various effect sizes. *Journal of Counseling Psychology, 51*(4), 473–481.

Ward, B. W. (2013). What's better—R, SAS, SPSS, or Stata? Thoughts for instructors of statistics and research methods courses. *Journal of Applied Social Science, 7*(1), 115–120.

Watkins, D. C. (2006). The depressive symptomatology of Black college men: Preliminary findings. *Californian Journal of Health Promotion, 4*(3), 187–197.

Watkins, D. C. (2012). Qualitative research: The importance of conducting research that doesn't "count." *Health Promotion Practice, 13*(2), 153–158.

Watkins, D. C., Green, B. L., Goodson, P., Guidry, J., & Stanley, C. A. (2007). Using focus groups to explore the stressful life events of black college men. *Journal of College Student Development, 48*(1), 105–118.

Watkins, D. C., & Neighbors, H. W. (2007). An initial exploration of what "mental health" means to young Black men. *Journal of Men's Health and Gender, 4*(3), 271–282.

Watkins, D. C., Rivers, D., Rowell, K., Green, B. L., & Rivers, B. M. (2006). A closer look at effect sizes and their relevance to health education. *American Journal of Health Education, 37*(2), 103–108.

Weinbach, R. W., & Grinnell, R. M. (2009). *Statistics for social workers* (8th ed.). Boston, MA: Allyn & Bacon.

Weinbach, R. W., & Grinnell, R. M. (2014). *Statistics for social workers* (9th Ed.). Boston, MA: Allyn & Bacon.

Wells, K. (2011). *Narrative inquiry.* New York, NY: Oxford University Press.

Wittink, M. N., Barg, F. K., & Gallo, J. J. (2006). Unwritten rules of talking to doctors about depression: Integrating qualitative and quantitative methods. *Annals of Family Medicine, 4*(4), 302–308.

Index

CPSIA information can be obtained at www.ICGtesting.com
Printed in the USA
BVOW02s1830200416

444842BV00007B/4/P